BLOGGING

Essential Guide

Antonia Chitty &
Erica Douglas

Blogging – The Essential Guide is also available in accessible formats for people with any degree of visual impairment. The large print edition and eBook (with accessibility features enabled) are available from Need2Know. Please let us know if there are any special features you require and we will do our best to accommodate your needs.

First published in Great Britain in 2012 by
Need2Know
Remus House
Coltsfoot Drive
Peterborough
PE2 9BF
Telephone 01733 898103
Fax 01733 313524
www.need2knowbooks.co.uk

Contents

Introduction

Welcome to *Blogging – The Essential Guide*. This book is for you if you have heard about blogging but want more information before you take the plunge, or if you have started a blog but feel that you need some help and guidance to understand all about making it a success. In this book we will guide you through the essentials of blogging and help you learn through clear explanations, examples and case studies.

In chapter 1, you can get to grips with 'blogging basics'. Read about what exactly a blog is, why different people write blogs, and how to pick a topic for your blog. You will learn about personal blogs, hobby blogs, business blogs and even how to blog professionally. We'll also share different people's opinions on what they believe makes a successful blog.

Chapter 2 shows you how to 'start a blog'. You can learn about different blog providers such as WordPress, Blogger and Typepad. Discover the difference between free and paid-for blogs, stand-alone blogs and those integrated into another website. Get to grips with posts and pages, links and images, and you will be well equipped to start blogging. You can also read some inspiring ideas to help you keep blogging and stay motivated.

Next, read chapter 3 to learn some essential online skills and concepts. You will learn some technical terms and quick tricks to get your blog off to a flying start. If HTML and SEO are just confusing acronyms right now, this chapter will help you understand what you need to know, and what you do not need to worry about.

In chapter 4, you can learn all about solutions to one of the most common problems for a blogger: getting fresh ideas. You will learn about concepts, such as mind mapping, to help you create a continual stream of new content for your blog. You can also read about how often to post and get to grips with different types of posts such as lists posts, reviews and memes, using images, vlogging and podcasting.

Unlike keeping a diary, interaction and being part of a community is a key element of blogging. Writing your own blog can help you link up with like-minded people. In chapter 5, learn about blog etiquette and writing comments. Discover blog carnivals and other ways to get involved with the blogging community. Find out why RSS (really simple syndication) can help you get readers, and get lots of other ways to promote your blog.

Chapter 6 explains the differences between writing for the Internet and for print. Some people are happy to just blog, but if you want to improve what you write, read this chapter to learn about style and structure for successful blogging. Surprisingly, people read in a different way when they are looking at content on a computer or phone compared to in print. How you write and structure your content can make it easier for people to read. You will also get a quick guide to common abbreviations used in online communications, plus a quick guide to grammar for non-writers.

There are some legal facts that you need to be clear about when blogging. Put simply, you can't copy other people or businesses' writing or images without permission. Read all about this in chapter 7, Writing a Blog and the Law.

In chapter 8 we'll show you how your blog can lead on to something bigger. Whether you want to create an eBook or eCourse, this chapter will show you what to do.

Chapter 9 will help you if you want more people to start interacting with your blog. In 'Social Media for Bloggers' you can learn how blogging is more fun if you link your blog into Twitter and Facebook, and how sites like LinkedIn and Ecademy can help your blog help your business.

Finally, chapter 10 explains how to make a profit from your blog. This works well if you have become keen on blogging and want a return for the time and efforts that you invest. Learn about monetising a blog, paid blogging, advertising on your blog, online feature writing, selling books and eBooks and affiliate schemes.

In every chapter you will find practical action steps to help you go from blogging beginner to brilliant blogger.

Chapter 1

Blogging Basics

What is a blog?

A blog is a type of website. The word 'blog' is a derivative from the words 'web log' describing a website written as a journal or diary. The first ever blogs were developed in the early 90s and since then the blogging phenomenon has taken off. Nowadays, there are millions of blogs on every topic you can think of. Blogs have become as much visited as some of their website counterparts and some bloggers are treated as members of the media, invited on press trips and made privy to breaking news.

Many people often wonder what makes a blog different from a standard website. On a blog the content is updated regularly with daily or weekly entries. These entries are called 'posts'. The latest posts appear nearest the top of the homepage and work backwards in date order down the page. There is also now a trend for magazine-style layouts whereby the page is split into sections highlighting different topics. Older posts are archived and a tagging system where posts are allocated 'name tags' according to their topic is used to help readers find older content that is relevant to them. A blog can be maintained and updated by one person or a team of writers.

Blogs differ from websites in that they usually have a built-in level of interactivity. Readers can leave comments on the blog posts allowing a two-way interaction between reader and publisher.

Blogs can simply be online diaries or they can be focused on a specific topic such as a hobby or business. Tightly focused blogs on a specific topic are often called niche websites and these sites are usually launched with strategies so that the site can make money from the outset.

Blogs receive an above average amount of traffic because search engines love the regular addition of fresh content. Couple this with the relaxed style and interactivity of most blogs, and it is a winning combination for both attracting traffic and turning that traffic into loyal readers.

Some bloggers go on to sell advertising space on their sites, write sponsored posts or sell products and services relevant to their audience.

Why blog?

People blog for many reasons. The majority of blogs start as a personal diary of parenthood, of weight loss, of a hobby or just of life in general. As the blogger continues to write, trends and themes may emerge or the blog may remain a diary of someone's life.

Your blog can be something you tell the world about, but you can also blog anonymously. Think about what you might like to write about. Is it something relatively personal and private to share with close friends and family, or a place where you can write incognito? This can affect the way you set up your blog (see chapter 2) and the name you choose for it.

Some people blog to earn money or raise the profile of their business. Blogs with the specific purpose of earning money will occupy very tight niches, provide high quality information and the owners will be focused on the pursuit of making money from the traffic to the site. Sites like these can be monetised by selling products, advertising and affiliate marketing. A new and developing trend is that of the 'business blog'. This is a blog that has posts based on topics relating to the business. Business blogs are used to increase customer loyalty, further cement the brand as a communication tool and to help potential customers find the business via search engines. Creative professionals – writers, artists and those wanting to break into these fields – will find a blog a great outlet to record and showcase their creative output.

Reasons to blog

People blog for many different reasons. Here are some ideas for different types of blog:

'Antonia says, "I started blogging at www.family friendlyworking. co.uk after I had written a book of the same name. I was still coming across interesting information, news and events for parents interested in flexible working and added them to the blog".'

Personal blogs

Many, many people start to blog as a personal online diary. People start at periods of change in their life and when they want to document a particular stage. This is why there are so many parenting bloggers, plus a number of people blogging the run-up to their weddings. Beyond that, you also find people blogging weight loss journeys or their thoughts as they battle illness.

When writing this sort of diary, you need to think about your own privacy, as well as that of the people you might mention in your posts. Most blog providers have options so that you can keep some posts private or only allow certain approved readers. You can blog anonymously – many people create a blogging name or identity and also give identities to the people they mention in their blog. You might make up names or use initials.

Hobby blogs

Do you have a hobby that you love? Blogging is a great way to share your experiences and tips and link up with other people with a similar interest. It allows you to make contact with enthusiasts across the globe, however focused and specialised your area of interest. This sort of blog can cover food, all sorts of craft, and sometimes technology or travel. There can be an overlap as people start blogging for (and about) a hobby then find they can blog for profit, either by selling advertising space, linking to products relevant to their hobby via an affiliate scheme, or even being paid to write on their specialist topic.

Business blogs

If you have a business, a blog can bring many benefits. It is a place to showcase what you offer and give people more of an insight into what you do. A business blog can help businesses build relationships with new and existing customers and it has many benefits as a way of increasing website traffic.

Anyone with a creative or professional profile can find business benefits too. A blog allows you to showcase your expertise and interact with people who could become followers or fans, clients or customers. Your blog can be a showcase of what you offer, an online portfolio to show to agents or commissioning editors.

'Carol says, "Make it, Bake it gives me a chance to be creative and indulge in three of my favourite things, coffee, chocolate and cupcakes. It's also a place for other people to share their recipes and crafts, a bit like an online WI".'

Carol, Blogger, www.makeitbakeit. co.uk and www. dancewithoutsleeping. co.uk

And some people use their blog to showcase their skills as a blogger. Working as a professional blogger for other businesses who want the benefits of a blog but do not have the staff or expertise, is a flexible and interesting career. Your own blog is the first step towards working in this area.

Why people start blogs

- @sallyanntodd – I started my blog because a friend suggested it in order to expand on my funny Facebook status updates!
- @benbloggerdad – I posted excerpts of a book I was writing to gauge reaction and see whether it was worth carrying on!
- @Ellen27 – As a treat. It was a little break from writing what other people wanted me to.
- @cambridgemummy – Because everyone else was and I wanted to find something to replace my teenage diary as a way of getting everything out of my system.
- @exmoorjane – A vain attempt to sell our house . . . :)
- @surprisedzoe – To celebrate a pregnancy that wasn't well received.

Choosing a topic

The first step to starting a blog is deciding what you will write about. Blogs cover all subjects, and I mean all subjects. Go to Google and search for any topic with 'blog' after it and you will find a blog covering that topic. Some of the most successful blogs are in the tiniest of niches. I just tested my own theory and went to Google and searched for 'dog medicine blog' and this was about the fourth listing: www.bark-n-blog.com.

Erica says, 'I started off as a 'mummy blogger' but do not let that tag put you off, most mummy bloggers spend the majority of their time blogging about everything other than parenting. I like to think of my blog more about my life as a parent rather than purely about parenting.'

'American mominengland. com writes, "I blog because it allows me to express myself in a way that I simply wasn't otherwise doing. Blogging allows me to express all my triumphs and frustrations with friends and family all around the world. It lets me sit and clarify how I feel about life. It keeps me connected when I'm feeling isolated and lost".'

An alternative approach is to simply start writing your blog and see what topic you feel like writing about that day. You may see something in the media or have something happen that spurs you on to write or rant. With time, a trend may emerge. See chapter 2 for more on how to get ideas to write about.

Whatever you decide to blog about, make sure you have plenty to say because there is nothing worse than starting a blog and finding you can only write half a dozen posts on the subject before exhausting your knowledge or sickening yourself of the topic. Thousands of blogs are started each year and then abandoned within days, weeks or months. Think about why you want to start a blog and remind yourself of this if you find yourself leaving long gaps between posts.

Choosing a name

Choosing a name for your blog can be quite a personal thing: choose something that you like, but also consider a name that represents yourself and what you plan to write about. There is no harm in asking others what springs to mind when you say the name. You could even consider asking other bloggers for their advice.

Erica says, 'My blog is called littlemummy.com because I'm rather short!'

Here are some of the blogs we read . . .

- Englishmum – so called because she's English.

- You've Got Your Hands Full – this blogger has twins and has probably heard this phrase a zillion times.

- Shinyshiny.tv is a blog about gadgets aimed at women.

- Badscience.net is the blog of Ben Goldacre who has written a column of the same name in the Guardian.

Choose something that is easy for your readers to remember. As a new blogger you need people to remember you if you are to gain a strong readership. Including a key word or phrase in your domain name can help you rank better in search engines. Try to avoid hyphens, difficult spellings and domains longer than 35 characters in length. Make it as easy as possible for people to find you.

What makes a successful blog?

There are many, many 'blog rankings' which rate the most 'successful' blogs. You can find these at sites including:

www.technorati.com/blogs/top100

www.blogstorm.co.uk/top-100-uk-blogs/

www.uk.cision.com/Resources/Social-Media-Index/Top-UK-Social-Media/

This sort of ranking takes into account a range of factors. First, the sites must be blogs – see 'what is a blog' at the start of the chapter. Some blog ranks are geographically based and will rank top blogs on certain topics in the UK only, for example. The blog's 'influence' is then measured, weighing up data including:

- Number of unique visitors.
- Page rank.
- Incoming links.
- Search engine results.
- Frequency of updates.
- Total number of posts.
- Number of comments.
- Engagement via social media sites including Twitter and Facebook.

Different rankings will give different weight to different factors. Some are influenced by other rankings such as Google Blogsearch and Klout results. Does ranking well on one of these charts equal success? Probably not for the majority of bloggers. Here are some more ideas about what makes a successful blog:

- If you are writing on a topic that you love, your success might be realised when you find you are playing an active part in a community of people who have the same passion for the topic as you.
- If you are writing a personal blog as a stay-at-home mum about the ups and downs of parenting life, you may feel that you have succeeded when PRs start contacting you and offering you baby products to review.

- If you are writing a blog to promote your creative output, such as a book, you may be aiming for the success of achieving a book deal.

Here are some more ideas from bloggers about how they feel about success:

@SurprisedZoe – 'When the people who comment seem to get me. That is when my blog is a success.'

'An outlet to write more information for my customers and try and turn visitors into customers.' Kerri of www.buystudentart.co.uk

@bigmelsblog_com – 'Starting and writing a blog is daunting there is no doubt about it. The late nights sat at my laptop choosing topics, planning posts and writing articles can be hard work, especially when trying to keep a house tidy, get the kids to school and be at your day job on time. I first felt my blog was successful when I got my first comment. It was from a friend granted but it meant the world to me that someone was interested in what I had to say. I write from the heart and sometimes tackle subjects that others would avoid like the plague, but I'm always reminded that people are out there and waiting for your posts and articles which may really brighten up their day or strike a chord or simply fill a gap in a topic they are interested in when I get a tweet, comment or email from a reader. Listeners are the success we should be striving for'.

@cambridgemummy – 'When people say "I sat there nodding/laughing/crying/smirking reading X". Lets me know I'm not on my own in the parenting malarky :).'

'People have said I should write only for myself, but if I didn't care about other people reading my stuff, I'd just write a diary. For me, successful blogging is all about the debate. I want to know that I've made you think, even if you passionately disagree with me. And to know I've done that, you need to leave me a comment'. Henrietta of www.marketingtomilk.WordPress.com

'Of course things like lots of traffic make me feel my blog is successful, but what I really love seeing are comments and discussions between the people who read the posts. Sometimes this happens on the blog but I also love seeing comment threads on Twitter or Facebook. It's important to know that people find what I post compelling enough to respond and react to it.' Jennifer of www.jenography.net

Quick action checklist

- Choose a topic.

- Choose a name.

- Think about why you want to blog.

- Decide if you will blog anonymously.

- Move on to chapter 2 and you will learn how to get started.

Summing Up

- If you are new to blogging, it is not complicated. A blog is simply an online diary. You might use it to jot down thoughts on life or to write about particular experiences or hobbies. Some people use blogs to earn money in their spare time, while business owners might blog to promote their business.

- If you want to start blogging, think about what you might write about. Is your blog going to be focused on a particular topic? Or do you just want to start writing and see what topics crop up? Will your blog be anonymous or will you link it to your other online profiles such as Facebook? Whatever you decide to do, take some time to choose a memorable name for your blog.

- Different people blog for different reasons and unless you are very competitive, appearing at the top of a blog ranking is not likely to be your main reason to blog. Think about why you are blogging, and what will make you feel that your blog is a success.

Chapter 2

Starting a Blog

In chapter 1 we looked at reasons why people blog and what makes a blog successful. In this chapter we look at information to help you start your blog.

Finding a blog provider

There are probably hundreds of different blog providers, but two stand out because of their popularity and functionality. Read on to find out more about Google Blogs, previously known as Blogger, and WordPress.

Google Blogs

If you are a beginner with no technical knowledge, blogging for pleasure or as a hobby, Google Blogs is a great place to start. It is free to start a Google Blogs blog, but your site is owned by Google.

There is a step-by-step guide available when you visit www.blogger.com and sign up to start a blog. You can get your blog off the ground in less than fifteen minutes. Anyone can use Google Blogs to set up a blog as long as they can use a mouse and can follow instructions. You can choose the appearance of your blog from a number of templates as part of the set-up process.

For professional bloggers, the disadvantage of using Google Blogs is that you do not own your own site. You can take advertisements using Adsense and use Amazon Associates as another way to monetise your site, but the company could close down your site at any time if they objected to your content, for example.

WordPress

WordPress offers two different options for blogging. WordPress.com and WordPress.org both come from the same company and use the same software.

WordPress.com sites are hosted and owned by WordPress. This means that all technical updates happen automatically, but again, you do not own your site.

With WordPress.org you need to install the software on your own server or with hosting provided for you by another company.

WordPress.com is great for you when you have little or no technical knowledge and need something easy and simple to set up fast, with the confidence that all the upgrades will be done for you. WordPress.com is hosted by WordPress which gives you less control, but their hosting seems reliable. It is free to use and ideal if you are blogging as a personal diary or for a hobby, or are a beginner blogger who wants to showcase your business.

WordPress.com

Benefits:

- It is free and much easier to set up than WordPress.org.
- Everything is taken care of: set-up, upgrades, spam, backups, security, etc.
- Your blog is on hundreds of servers, so it is unlikely it will go down if you have a lot of visitors.
- Your posts are backed up automatically.
- You get extra traffic from blogs of the day and tags.
- You can find like-minded bloggers using tag and friend surfer.
- Your login is secure (SSL) so no one can get into your account if you use Wi-Fi.

Cons:

- You cannot run a custom theme (that is what affects how your site looks) without joining the VIP programme.

- You can't customise the PHP code behind your blog without joining the VIP programme – this affects integrating some ways to make money like affiliate schemes and payment buttons from some providers.

- You can't upload plugins without joining the VIP programme.

- No adverts allowed.

Overall, WordPress.com is a great place to start and can be all you need for a hobby blog. It may become frustrating and drive you to upgrade if you are serious about customising your blog or making a living from blogging.

WordPress.org is for you if you want total control! You can change the way your site appears and add in all sorts of widgets and plugins.

Unless you have good technical knowledge you will need to get help with set-up but you get the same easy-to-use control panel as with WordPress.com and can update the site yourself. It is the best system if you want to monetise your site.

Using WordPress.org is slightly more complicated and costly than using Google Blogs or WordPress.com. You will need to arrange your own hosting and domain name.

Purchasing a domain name from the likes of www.123 reg.co.uk or www.1and1.co.uk is simple: many of these companies can also provide hosting as part of a package or you can search for 'hosting providers'.

WordPress.org

Benefits:

- You can upload themes to change the appearance of your site.

- You can upload all sorts of plugins which gives much more scope for what you can do with the site, from simple widgets to full shopping cart systems.

- Complete control to change code if you are technically minded.

Cons:

- You need a good web host, which you will have to pay for. Hosting costs are a few pounds a month to start but can increase if you have lots of traffic.

- You need more technical knowledge.

- You are responsible for stopping spam.

- You have to handle backups.

- You must upgrade the software manually when a new version comes out.

- If you get a huge spike in traffic, for example from a plug on the front page of a site like Digg your hosting needs to be able to cope.

Where to start?

If you are unsure, start with www.WordPress.com and all your input and work can be transferred across to a www.WordPress.org site at a later stage or once you start feeling the limitations of what you can do. You can also start a blog on Google Blogs and transfer all your content to WordPress.org later on, but this is a little more complex. Some bloggers wish in hindsight that they had started on their own domain name from the outset. WordPress.com is a good option if you are just trying blogging out or you can't afford the costs involved in purchasing, hosting and a domain name right now.

The most important thing is to make a start. Blogging is for everyone, so do not let lack of money or technical knowledge hold you back.

NB: This book is not a guide to the technicalities of setting up a blog. You may be technical and do it yourself or have a friend that can do it for you. If not then you can pay someone a one-off fee to do this for you. For a few hundred pounds they will deal with your set-up and customise your theme.

More blog host options

* LiveJournal
* Dreamwidth
* InsaneJournal
* Bravenet.com
* TypePad
* Squarespace
* Movable Type

Choosing a look for your blog

In Google Blogs, the look of your blog, the bit your readers see, is called a 'template'. In WordPress it's called a 'theme'. In Google Blogs you choose your template from a selection that you are offered during their step-by-step process. For WordPress.org simply search for WordPress themes in Google and a selection will come up, some free and some which you can buy.

If you are getting help to create your WordPress site, your webmaster may be able to advise you on your choice of theme; some themes are better for customisation, others may be great for SEO. A web professional will also be able to customise your theme, but this will cost more.

When you choose the look of your blog, you need to weigh up how people will use it as well as what appeals visually. Think about:

Layout

Look at a number of blogs and you will see that some have two columns, while others have three or even four. Some may have a panel at the top with a featured post or image. You need to make it easy for people to find their way around the site, consider how many different post titles or extracts will be visible before people have to scroll down the page, for example. Consider what you might need to have in the side bars of your site:

- Links to other blogs.

- Advertisements.

- Products for sale.

- A sign-up box for an eCourse or newsletter.

- A search box.

- Lists of pages.

- Lists of tags or a tag cloud.

- Categories.

- Lists of recent posts.

- Lists of recent comments.

The best way to decide on your layout is to examine other blogs and note down features that appeal to you. Then, browse available themes and see what matches your needs. Do not feel you have to get it right first time, many bloggers change the appearance of their site more than once as it evolves.

Colour

Once you have some ideas about layout, consider the colour you'd like for your blog. By all means pick your favourite colours; it is after all *your* blog. If you have a business, consider the colours people usually associate with it; see the next section on branding too. Some colour combinations are easier to read than others. For example, many people find it uncomfortable to read white text on a black background. Here are some more associations with colour:

- Pink: youth, for girls, fun, frivolous, weddings, babies.

- Red: fast, hot, love, blood.

- Orange: happiness, warmth.

- Yellow: bright, wellbeing, cheerful.

- Green: natural, healthy, eco-friendly.

- Blue: calm, clean, fresh.

- Black: modern, intense, youth, death, serious.
- Grey: serious, businesslike, dull.
- White: marriage (in Western cultures), death (in Eastern cultures).

Branding

Once you have started thinking about the appearance of your blog, you have taken the first steps in creating a brand for your site. Here are some more ideas for different types of blog:

Personal blogs

A personal blog gives you lots of scope for being really creative. Consider how you will make your site personal to you. Add a customised logo in your header or a picture in the sidebar. Remember there are millions of blogs so try and make yours a little unique and memorable if possible.

Hobby blogs

Your hobby blog will also be a great starting place to create a strong visual brand. Take photos of your hobby until you find one that really sums it up then adapt it to create a banner that includes the name of your blog and use it as a header. This is the sort of image you might like to incorporate into your favicon, your gravatar (see chapter 3), and any banner ads you create for your site.

Business blogger

If you have a business, it should have a strong visual identity already. (If not, see *Marketing – The Essential Guide*, Need2Know Books for advice on branding your business). Make sure that your blog is as sympathetic as possible to your main website. Some businesses make the blog part of the main site, which has maximum benefits for SEO and attracting traffic and also

'Erica says, "At one stage I had a rotating header on my parenting blog that featured a few pictures of my daughter and things we'd done".'

ensures that the visual image is not an issue. If you have a stand-alone blog, invest in getting it customised to match your main site, unless you are using it to attract a new and different audience.

Blogging for your expert profile – authors, creative, artists

If you are a creative artist, make sure that your work is a strong visual presence in your site. Include a key piece in your header and consider using a plugin in the sidebar to allow you to display a gallery of your work.

Professional blogger

As a professional blogger, you will want to keep your blog as a professional showcase. Consider the colours you use in this light and consider if you need to develop a professional brand. Layout is vital. Make sure that it is easy for potential clients to find examples of your work and testimonials, as well as how to get in touch with you.

Writing posts and pages

So, you have a shiny new blog looking just how you want it, all ready to go. What you need now, is some content. In this section you can learn about writing your first post and creating pages.

Your first post

Sometimes it can be hard to decide on those first words for your blog. Why not start with a welcome post? Explain who you are, why you are blogging and what readers can expect from the blog. Remember that this post will remain on your site until you delete it, so make sure that it will still be relevant in a few months or years.

How to write a post in Google Blogs (Blogger)

1. Sign in to your blog.

2. Go to the dashboard area of your blog.

3. Click on the 'new post' link.

4. You will now see your posting area; write your blog post in the large white area. You can experiment with the B (bold), I (italic), U (underlined) buttons to change the appearance of what you write.

5. Give it a title – just write in the 'title' box.

6. Write 'labels' for your post. These are the keywords or 'tags' to describe the topics you have covered.

7. Once you are happy with what you have written, click the 'publish post' button.

How to write a post in WordPress

1. Go to the dashboard area of your blog.

2. Click on 'new post'. Write your post onto the blank page.

3. Give your post some tags. These are just keywords about what the post is about. At this point you may also want to choose a few categories that tie in with the themes you will be writing about regularly. You can add categories at any point, but it is better to plan them than to keep adding and adding at random.

4. Once you are happy click 'publish'. Your post will appear on the 'front screen' of your blog.

Pages

Pages are different to posts in structure, but written in much the same way. Blog posts are usually displayed with the most recent post at the top of a page full of blog posts. In your blog control panel or dashboard you will find two options where you can opt to create and manage 'pages' or to create and manage 'posts'. It is easy to mix the two up: why not go and check that you can find each area in your own blog now. Check each time that you are writing a post or page that you are in the right place.

Use 'pages' to cover timeless content that people will want to refer to regularly, such as 'about', 'contact', 'advertise', 'press' and 'newsletter' pages.

Read on for more ideas for what to include in your pages:

About

The first place to start, almost every blogger has an 'about' page. Use it to tell your readers about you, your blog and why it exists. Include a photo unless you want to keep your blog anonymous.

If you are blogging for business on a stand-alone blog, link to your main business site; if your blog is integrated you will probably have an 'about the business' page already.

Contact

Do you want people to get in touch with you? If so, make it easy by having a 'contact' page. Some blogs have an inbuilt contact template or, in WordPress, download the wp-contactform template. You can just include your email address for readers to contact you, but a contact page form can provide an additional layer of protection from spam.

Advertise, Press, Newsletter pages

As your blog grows, you can add in further pages. If you want to earn through advertising, explain how people can advertise with a page dedicated to the topic. If you get media coverage for your site, add that to a 'press' page, which can also include details of who to contact for media comments or reviews. If you compile your blog posts into a newsletter, create a page so people can get what you write direct to your inbox. You can learn more about this later in the book.

What other pages have you seen on other sites? Which ones might be useful to you? Start planning whether you might need terms and conditions if you are selling via your website or running competitions. Here are some more ideas; tick ones that you might need:

More ideas for pages

- Terms and conditions.
- Privacy policy.
- Awards.
- Groups you belong to.
- Frequently asked questions.
- Press releases.
- Testimonials.
- Links.

Links and images

Once you have understood the basics of creating a post or page, you will want to add links and images to everything you create in your blog. Images improve the appearance of your blog and can attract readers. Links are needed so you can give credit when you quote someone or mention something. You need to learn how to link to other blogs and websites to do this.

Links

If you are planning on writing about something that is mentioned on another blog or website, you need to link to your source. This is both good etiquette, and also allows your readers to follow up on what you have blogged about.

How to link

This works for most blogging systems:

1. Highlight the words you wish to use as the link. Pick the words that describe what people will click on to, rather than 'click here'. See chapter 4 for more on this.

2. Click the 'link' button just above your posting area which may appear as an icon with a chain on it, or an icon with a globe with a chain in it. A pop-up box will appear.

3. Paste the URL (web address) into the space in the pop-up box. Make sure you include the http:// part of the web address.

4. Your chosen words should now appear highlighted and should link to the website when you click on them.

5. Check your links before publishing. Use the 'preview' function so you can read through your post and click on the links.

There is more about what makes a 'good' link in chapter 4.

Images

Images make a big difference to your blog. Aim to use at least one image per post. Sometimes you may want the image to be the main focus for the post. Here are a few steps to help you upload great images to your blog:

1. Prepare your photo. If you have a very large image, reduce it in size before uploading to make blogging faster and easier for you and your readers. This is also the stage where you can get rid of red eye or deal with any other issues with the original image, using a programme such as Photoshop, Paint or Picasa.

2. Next, go into your dashboard. If you have a particular post that you are working on in WordPress, you will find an 'upload image' button above the main controls for text formatting. If you want to upload an image for future use, you can also find your 'media library' in the sidebar of your dashboard and simply click 'add new'.

3. A pop-up will appear. Click 'browse' to find the file, double click on your desired photo, and you will be taken back to the original box. Click 'upload'.

4. Now, create a title and caption for your image. If you are uploading within a post, decide where the photo should go; 'left', 'centre', or 'right'. Make your choices and click 'insert into post' or 'upload image' and your post should now feature your photo.

See chapter 4 for tips on finding images to use.

Quick action checklist

▪ Look at different blog providers and choose one that suits you.

▪ Create your first 'page'. An 'about' page is a good place to start.

▪ Start planning some ideas for posts. See chapter 4 for more ideas on how to do this.

▪ Practise writing your first post and insert an image.

Summing Up

- Follow the content in this chapter and you will have gone from choosing a blog provider to having your blog up and running. There are lots of pros and cons to different providers: hobby and personal bloggers with basic needs can start simple with Google Blogs or WordPress.com, while anyone with a business or who is looking to earn from their blog should use WordPress.org which requires you to invest in hosting and a domain name.

- Take time to create the right appearance for your blog, you do not have to get this right first time so feel free to experiment with different 'templates' or 'themes'. Ask readers for views too!

- Practise writing your first post, to explain why you have started blogging and learn how to create pages such as your 'about' page and your 'contact' page. Insert an image and a link to your first post or page, and you will have covered many blogging basics. Now move on to chapter 3 which will give you some blogging basics that will help you build your skills.

Chapter 3

Basic Online Skills and Concepts

A lot of blogging is about getting onto the computer, signing up for a free blog and giving it a go. You can learn an enormous amount of what you need to know about blogging simply by experimentation and intuition. However, there are some quick tricks and handy things to know and understand that will give you a head start. Read through this chapter quickly, then get on to your blog and put what you have learnt into practice.

You've got the power!

The Internet has made an enormous difference to what we read and the media we consume every day. Even as little as 10 years ago, if you wanted to rant about something you could tell your friends or write to the company concerned. Now, your rant can have an audience of millions if it hits a nerve and covers a topic that lots of others are looking for. In the past, if you were first on the scene of an accident or disaster, your views might be communicated to others via an intermediary if you spoke to a journalist who then published your comments in a newspaper. Now you can post what is happening on your blog, Twitter or Facebook and everyone can get the news as it happens. And anyone can contribute their views to debates on fora, or make comments at the end of blog posts too.

This is known as user generated content, and is transforming the 21st century. As a blogger, you can be part of that transformation and write great content to share with people who are interested in the topic that you are writing on. If you

'A lot of blogging is about getting onto the computer, signing up for a free blog and giving it a go.'

always aspired to be a journalist, you can run your own magazine in miniature on your blog, or even set up your own publishing company with multiple websites or eBooks on offer.

Feeling inspired to start blogging? Here are some quick tips to give you a fast start. If you have been blogging for a while you might also find that these tips help you make sense of things that have been unclear!

Basic HTML

Do you know how to add bullets, underlining or other structure to what you write in your blog? Hypertext mark up language (HTML) is the code that creates websites, and understanding a little about it will help you with your blogging.

To start with though, take a look at the control panel which you can find on the top of the space where you can create a post or page in WordPress. We are using WordPress as an example, but you will find similar panels in other blogging systems.

This panel of buttons allows you to click and create a range of styles for your text, including bold, italics etc. When you write a post in WordPress or Blogger, this panel can take care of the HTML for you. However you may want to use HTML manually, for example when commenting and being able to identify what code is having what effect can make it easier to remove bits.

Here are some examples and the code you need to create them:

---

bold
bold

Italic
italic

Underlined
underlined

```
■ bullet points

■ bullet points

■ bullet points

<ul>
<li>bullet points</li>
<li>bullet points</li>
<li>bullet points</li>
</ul>

align left
<p style="text-align: left;">align left</p>

                           centre
          <p style="text-align: center;">centre</p>

                                              align right
              <p style="text-align: right;">align right</p>
```

Linking

There are lots of reasons to include links in your blog posts and we'll talk more about this later in the book too. Basically, if you want to quote another blogger, it is good practice to include a link to their blog. The same applies if you are referring to a news article or other website; include a link to the source. Links in to your site can help it rise up the search engine rankings, so by linking to others you are helping them as well as telling your readers where to go to find out more about the article you mention. Overleaf you can see the HTML you need to insert a link: often though, you will find a 'link' button where you simply need to insert the website or page's URL.

```
www.need2knowbooks.co.uk
<a href="http://www.need2knowbooks.co.uk/">link</a></p>

You can link to a site's main page:
e.g. – http://www.need2knowbooks.co.uk/

or you can link to a specific page:
http://www.need2knowbooks.co.uk/marketing-the-essential-guide-ebook/

Go one stage further and you can use keywords to link to a site rather than
the site URL
e.g.
My books are published by Need 2 Know Books
My books are published by <a href="http://www.need2knowbooks.co.uk
/">Need 2 Know Books</a>

Or
Read Marketing the Essential Guide
Read <a href="http://www.need2knowbooks.co.uk/marketing-the-
essential-guide-ebook/">Marketing the Essential Guide</a>
```

If you have found some HTML that is puzzling you, simply Google it and you will often find an explanation. There is a lot more about HTML in easy lessons at: www.w3schools.com/html/default.asp.

Search engine optimisation

SEO stands for search engine optimisation. You need to know about SEO to ensure that people can find your website when they search for relevant terms in Google and other search engines. This may be very important for your blog, or not important at all – see Is SEO for you? on the next page.

Search engines use secret algorithm to rank blogs and all other websites. Although nobody knows the exact algorithm, there are some known ways to help people find your blog when they search. This is what search engine optimisation is all about.

Is SEO for you?

Personal blogs

If you are writing a blog as a personal journal, SEO is unlikely to be the top of your priorities. It can help other like-minded bloggers writing on the same topics find you. If you are writing a private and confidential blog and do not want to link up with other people, this knowledge may help you know what to avoid!

Hobby blogs

SEO can help if you want to attract more readers, either as an end in itself or as a way to help you make your hobby blog pay for itself through advertising.

Business blogs

SEO is important if you are blogging for your business. Use key phrases to bring in customers who are searching for the products or services that your business provides.

'SEO can help if you want to attract more readers.'

Blogging for your expert profile – authors, creative, artists

If you are blogging to raise your profile as an expert, devise a list of key terms and phrases that you would like to be found for. Note down where your site ranks currently on different search engines and make sure you use your phrases regularly to help your site be found more easily.

Professional blogger

Many clients will pay bloggers to write posts that focus on key words and phrases. Adding fresh content with the right keywords is a top strategy to help with SEO. What key words and phrases does your client want to be ranked for on search engines?

There are hundreds of SEO tactics and many sites devoted to the latest ways to work the system. You could spend many hours working on SEO, but if you are blogging for fun it slightly defeats the object. Even if you are blogging professionally, you do not need to know all about SEO to be able to write posts that will help your business or your client's business. Here are four ideas that you can easily put into practice improve your search engine rank:

1. Submit your URL to Google

   You can't rank if they do not even know you exist. Google will eventually find and rank your blog but submitting your URL ensures this happens at the earliest point.

2. Keywords

   Decide what keywords you'd like to rank for and use those keywords in the title and the body of your posts. For example, you have a cooking blog and you want to rank for 'cheese bread'. Make sure that you do several recipes for cheese bread and use 'cheese bread' in the title, and body of your post, and in your tags.(That is the words that you add at the end of the post in the 'tags' box that describe what the post is about.)

   Use keywords and phrases two to three times in a page or post. Do not overuse keywords or your blog can actually be penalised.

3. Good links

   When you link ensure that you create 'good' links. This means that the link itself relates to its destination. Here are three possible links to a post on littlemummy.com about Christmas gift ideas, with a brief explanation below each as to whether it's a good link. The underlined text is the link:

   Littlemummy has some good Christmas gift ideas – click here!

   If you give a link like this, Google will rank the Little Mummy blog for the terms 'click here', terms which are not of particular interest to anyone! The blog will not be found by people looking for 'Christmas gift ideas'.

   Littlemummy has some good Christmas gift ideas!

Using a link to the blog name or business name is marginally better than the previous example, but most sites will already rank well for their blog name or business name, so this sort of link doesn't add as much weight as the best example, below.

Littlemummy has some good Christmas gift ideas!

This is fantastic. Search engines like Google will recognise that you have linked to the Littlemummy blog for the key phrase 'Christmas gift ideas'. Now people searching for 'Christmas gift ideas' have a better chance of finding this post on the Littlemummy site. Hopefully their needs will be fulfilled and the site may gain a new reader.

4. Incoming Links

The more incoming links you receive from different websites the better your blog will rank on search pages. This is because Google and other search engines will see your blog as an authority on that topic. You need to attract as many incoming links as you can. The number one way to do this is through good content. If your content is good enough people will link to it. It really is as simple as that.

Take part in memes, competitions, writing workshops and other weekly features as they are great ways to attract links.

More SEO ideas

If you become interested in SEO, you will find lots more ways to increase the visibility of your site on search. Better search results will bring more readers. Here are some more ways to help you affect your ranking:

- Have your own domain name. E.g., www.yourblog.co.uk rather than yourblog.WordPress.com.

- Register your domain for the maximum available time.

- Link between your own posts using good keywords; this will draw search robots deeper into your site and help all your posts and pages rank.

How your blog looks

Themes

When you start blogging your blogs, visual image may not be at the forefront of your mind, but you will soon see other people with attractive blogs and want to make yours look as good as possible. When you set up your blog you will have a choice of themes that you can start with. A theme usually incorporates an image, a certain number of columns, a certain layout and colours, all creating a visual identity for your blog.

Some themes can be customised relatively simply and offer you a choice of colours or layouts, others can be customised if you have more technical knowledge. You can opt for free themes, which you will find used by many other bloggers, or upgrade to a paid theme with more options. Some themes are well designed to maximise SEO; others are designed for different purposes. Google a topic such as 'WordPress Themes' to get a better idea of the different appearances you can create for your blog.

'Favicon stands for "favourite icon".'

Favicons

Favicon stands for 'favourite icon'. It is a small image that you can see in the tab at the top of your browser when you visit a site. A favicon helps to promote a professional image for your site and make it more recognisable. You can create a favicon at: www.favicon.co.uk/. You can install your favicon yourself if you understand the HTML required, but you may want to get some technical help. There are instructions here: www.favicon.co.uk/help.php.

Gravatars

A key part of blogging is interacting with the blogging community and you can use a gravatar to make sure your visual image appears alongside what you write on almost any blog. Gravatar stands for globally recognized avatar – an avatar is simply a visual representation of a person.

If you look at comments on a blog, you will see that some people have pictures next to their name and some do not. To get a picture next to your comments, get a gravatar.

Getting your own gravatar is as easy as opening a free account with Gravatar and uploading your picture or logo; visit www.gravatar.com. If you do not get how it works watch the video on the front page, it explains it really well.

Quick action checklist

- Read about basic HTML.
- Learn a little about SEO and work out your key words.
- Use keywords in your next posts.
- Use good links in your posts.
- Set up your blog's theme.
- Create a favicon.
- Create a gravatar.

Summing Up

- There are lots of technical things to get to grips with when you start blogging, but you will find that actually it is all quite simple with a little practice. Most blog providers make it easy for you to use bold, underlining, italics and other layouts in your blog by just highlighting text and clicking a button. If you understand a little basic HTML you will also be able to create these effects by using code. Perhaps more importantly you will also understand how to remove code if you need to.

- Search engine optimisation is often seen as a dark art, but a little basic SEO knowledge is relatively simple to acquire and can help you attract more visitors to your site who are interested in the topics that you are writing about. Follow the tips in this chapter and you will have a good idea on what will help people find your posts and pages.

- The appearance of your blog can make it more attractive for readers and you can get an immense amount of satisfaction when your blog looks the way you want. Research themes that will give you different looks for your blog and add in a favicon and gravatar to make sure that you carry that image wherever your blog is seen.

Chapter 4

Content for Your Blog

In this chapter we are going to look at creating content for your blog. Many people find content creation daunting from the beginning. Others get off to a flying start and then run into problems later on when their initial ideas have been exhausted.

We are going to cover techniques to ensure that you always have a steady supply of ideas for blog posts. We'll also cover how to publish your first post along with how to create multi-media content. Read on to find out how to formulate and organise your ideas as the basis of a brilliant blog.

Getting ideas for content

You may have decided to start a blog because you have extensive knowledge in a particular area or you have lots of ideas that you need to 'get out there'. If this is the case, grab a pen and paper now and jot down all the ideas you currently have. This will allow you to clear your mind before you move on to the other exercises in this chapter. Also it will give you a good idea of where you are in terms of how much content you have inside you.

Jotting down ideas is a good habit to get into by the way, so you may want to invest in a notebook or download an app for your phone that allows you to capture ideas on the move.

Once you have exhausted all your initial ideas, take a pause. How many ideas do you have? You may have listed 20 ideas or 100. Whatever you have is fine. Review your ideas and see if you can pick out the three main topics they cover. If you have more than three then this is probably too wide a niche if you are blogging to make money or promote your business. If you are blogging for purely personal reasons then you can blog on whatever you like and coming up with widely varying ideas for blog posts is probably not a problem.

'Jotting down ideas is a good habit to get into.'

You should now be clear on what your three main sub-topics are. For example, if I was considering starting a pottery blog then my three sub-topics might be:

- Creating pottery.
- Designing and painting pottery.
- Selling my pottery.

These sub-topics ensure that the niche is narrow enough for me to attract readers from search engines and also to keep my readers interested, as presumably all three of those sub-topics will be of interest. If I had recipe ideas as one of my sub-topics, or film reviews, you can see how that would cause confusion for the reader. Search engines wouldn't know how to categorise my blog; they wouldn't understand what I was an 'authority' on.

Once you are clear on your niche you will find it much easier to come up with new ideas.

How to capture the ideas

We have already mentioned the virtues of a notebook or app for collecting ideas. The next phase is to create a blog post title from each idea. A practical title that reflects exactly what the post is about is best. Keep this list of blog post titles somewhere. Next time you are ready to blog you can simply pick one and start writing. If you feel that it would be helpful to add some main bullet points to each idea then you can do that too.

Getting more ideas

Once you have exhausted your initial list of ideas the real work begins. You now have to come up with regular brand new content. This is a sticking point for many bloggers but it doesn't have to be. Follow the simple exercise overleaf and you will be able to come up with endless ideas for content that never dilute your subject area.

The exercise we are about to cover uses mind mapping. If you are familiar with mind mapping then that is great. If not, you may want to search for 'mind map' in a search engine to familiarise yourself. Mind mapping is much the same as a spider diagram.

Start by writing your blog name in the centre of a large piece of paper:

Next create three to four 'arms' off the central blog name and add a topic title to each arm.

Create further arms off each of these sub-topics with blog post ideas.

Now, take each of these ideas and create further ideas, this ensures that you are going 'deeper' into a topic as opposed to diluting your blog with blog posts covering other topics.

See diagram overleaf for an example.

Frequency of posting

Now that you have an ongoing supply of blog post ideas, you may be wondering how often to post. This is entirely up to you and will depend on how often you want to spend time creating and publishing blog posts and how much time you have.

Search engines love fresh content so the more the better to build your search engine rankings. Your followers, however, may only be able to manage to read a post a day or a post every two days.

Choose a frequency that suits you, satisfies your readers to keep them returning to your blog and is frequent enough to develop your position for key search terms. We find that three to five posts a week works well for many blogs.

Scheduling posts

You can either choose to publish posts as the fancy takes you or you can schedule them. Scheduling means that you can arrange posts to be published automatically in advance. Go to the dashboard area of your blog, write your post and then edit the date stamp to a date in the future. You will then be given the option to 'schedule' instead of 'publish'.

'Search engines love fresh content.'

- Tips for creating your first time
- 10 top pottery mistakes
- Creating a vase that looks professional
- Advanced tips for creating great pottery

- Complementary colours to use
- Glazing effects like cracking
- Designing your first piece of pottery
- 5 popular pottery styles

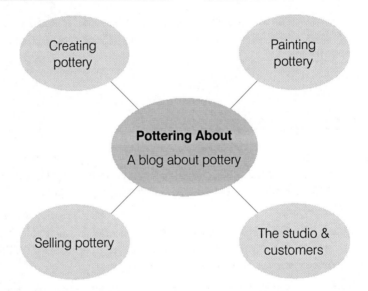

Creating pottery

Painting pottery

Pottering About
A blog about pottery

Selling pottery

The studio & customers

- How to create pottery to sell
- Where to sell your pottery
- How much to charge for your pottery
- What do pottery buyers want?
- How to start your own pottery business

- A video tour of the studio
- A podcast interview with Mr Potter (owner)
- FAQs about pottery
- Reviews from customers
- Staff features
- Slideshow of photos

If you want, you can go one step further and cover certain topics on different days so your blog schedule may be a 'tips' or 'how to' post on a Monday, a competition or picture post on a Wednesday and a multi-media post like a video or podcast on a Friday.

Scheduling can take a lot of the work out of blogging as you can schedule lots of posts when you are in the flow of writing and then take a break knowing that your posts are being automatically published.

Other ideas to include in your post

If you mention another blog or website or quote someone, it is helpful to the reader and good manners to give credit. For example: if you take a quote from another blog you need to provide a link to where the full article can be read.

Another helpful thing to do is provide sources for additional reading in your subject area: these can be other sites or other blogs posts that you have written on your own site.

Finally, make your post easy to read with lots of headings, breaks in paragraphs and bullet points. Some bloggers even choose to bold the main points for those who like to skim read.

Different types of posts

The way to ensure your blog remains engaging is to produce and publish lots of different types of content. Below are a number of different post ideas that you can apply to your niche that will keep your readers coming back for more.

List post

A top ten or similar on a specific topic.

Using the pottery example it could be 'Top ten most famous pieces of pottery'.

'The way to ensure your blog remains engaging is to produce and publish lots of different types of content.'

If you want to create content that people will link and share then go for the exhaustive list. For example: a Top 50 or Top 100. A post like this will not only be linked to and shared on social media sites, but if it's a practical list such as 'Top 50 Summer Activities for Kids' then your readers will refer to it again and again.

Discursive post

A discussion of the points for and against of a particular topic. A popular discursive topic could be breastfeeding Vs. bottle feeding, or Xbox Vs. PlayStation. Think what the controversial topics in your niche are then write an in-depth post with supporting evidence that displays both sides of the argument.

Posts like this tend to get a lot of comments so try and keep the discussion going by contributing in the comments area and responding to readers' views.

How-to

A post that teaches someone 'how to' do something.

If you have a gaming blog it might be 'How to win the league in FIFA', or 'How to make play dough' if you have a blog on children's activities. These posts are almost always enhanced by the use of photos and videos. This sort of post is ideal for hobby bloggers.

Story

A story post can be either fictional or real life. Stories are engaging, they are a good way of drawing people in and making them feel like they know you a little better.

Competition

Why not run a quiz or giveaway? A competition always attracts a good amount of interest. Have people enter by either commenting or 'retweeting' your post on Twitter. Create some terms and conditions for your competition before you run it. Can people only enter once? Do they need to be a resident in the UK or can you send a prize overseas? When does the competition close?

Survey/Poll

Embed a survey or poll into your blog post. You can do this via a site like www.SurveyMonkey.com.

Surveys and polls allow the reader to take another step in interacting with you and your blog. They can help you discover more about your readers and topics that they are interested in. This could be a source of more blog post ideas.

Recipe

Obviously this sort of post is only relevant if food or recipes are one of your sub-topics or related to your niche.

Picture

A picture with either no words at all or very few, maybe several photos. They say a good picture says a thousand words. Keep things fresh by including some photograph-only posts.

Review

This may be a paid or unpaid review of a game, an event, holiday destination, a restaurant; the list is endless. Choose something related to your niche to review.

Activity

A post of an activity that you have done. For example, if your blog is on extreme sports then it could be your latest cliff dive, or if you have a hill walking blog it could be a picture of you at the summit along with a few paragraphs of what it took to get there.

Case study/Report

A report about a particular topic or a case study of a business etc. We run a couple of 'women in business' blogs and one of the most popular features is the new business case studies. Consider your own niche and what might make an interesting case study or report.

News/Update

This can be personal news, business news, or general news in your niche. Think about what your readers would find interesting and newsworthy and create a post about it.

Slideshow

A post with a slideshow embedded. You can create a slideshow using Picasa or Smilebox. This is ideal if you have lots of images on a topic; if you run a travel blog perhaps.

Podcast

A post with a podcast embedded into it (how to podcast is covered later in this chapter). Your podcast could simply feature you talking on your niche topic, or you could take it one step further and interview an expert or someone interesting in your niche.

Vlog

A post with a video in it (how to create and upload a video will be covered later in this chapter). Create your own video tour, interview or how-to. Be as creative as you can.

Interview

You could interview a staff member, a customer, another blogger or someone famous.

Images

Embellish your posts with well-chosen images. Pictures really help to capture the reader's imagination and draw them in to read the words on the screen, a difficult thing to do when there is so much 'noise' and competition for attention. You can use your own personal images, images that have a 'creative commons' licence on Flickr (follow the steps below) or you can purchase photos from somewhere like iStockphoto.

To use photos from Flickr:

1. Go to Flickr (www.flikr.com) and create a free account.

2. On the front page, in the right hand corner click on 'search', then click on 'advanced search'.

3. Insert a keyword or two for the type of picture you are looking for. Scroll down and check the box that says 'only search within creative commons-licensed content'. Then click 'search'.

4. Once you have found a picture, click on 'all sizes' which is just above it. Choose a size and save to your computer.

5. Give credit at the foot of your post. I usually put 'Photo by Flickr user (name)' and link the name directly to the photo in Flickr.

6. Leave a comment on Flickr beneath the post thanking the person for the photo and leaving a link to where you used it. This is good manners, and many people have contacted me and thanked me for using their photo when I have commented like this.

'Pictures really help to capture the reader's imagination and draw them in to read the words on the screen.'

Podcasting

A podcast is an audio file that can be embedded into a blog post allowing your readers to listen. They can also download the audio file to an iPod, iPhone or any other MP3 player and listen on the move.

Why podcast?

A podcast is great as it allows your readers to consume your content in a different way and even away from their computer altogether.

What to podcast?

You could simply record yourself talking on a specific topic, however an interview makes for a great podcast.

How to podcast?

You can do this by simply recording yourself using your computer, however if you want the ability to edit your audio file you will need to download free software online called 'audacity', this will record your voice and allow you to embed music and cut and edit it where necessary. Spend a while messing around with it as that is the best way to get to grips with it. To set up an interview you can use Skype along with recording software such as 'Pamela'. Once you are happy you can use the WordPress podcast plugin to embed into your blog post and upload your podcast to iTunes.

Video (vlogging)

Video blogging or 'vlogging' is popular at the moment; it is also getting much easier to do with affordable, high quality digital cameras widely available and easy-to-use software. Most cameras have a USB built in and they carry their own software. To upload a video you simply need to plug it into your laptop or

PC. Once you have finished filming you can also cut and edit your video using the in-built software. Then save it to your computer. Once you are ready to share your footage you can upload to a video sharing site like YouTube.

Uploading to YouTube

1. Open a YouTube account if you do not already have one.
2. Click 'upload' to upload a video straight from your computer.
3. Use the 'embed' code to display it on your blog.

Quick action checklist

The main points from this chapter.

- Create a list of all the blog post ideas you currently have.
- Create blog post titles from all your ideas.
- Use mind mapping to come up with fresh content ideas.
- Go 'deeper' into your niche rather than diluting it with irrelevant content.
- Decide on a posting frequency and stick to it.
- Consider having a blog schedule and posting blog posts in advance.
- Maintain interest in your blog by writing different types of posts.
- Use images to illustrate your blog posts.
- Create multi-media like podcasts and videos.

Summing Up

- That brings us to the end of this chapter on creating content for your blog. I hope you are inspired and can see how easy it is to create engaging content regularly and ongoing. Now you need to work on the niche for your blog, and then start expanding from this tightly focused area and discover all the different areas within the topic that you could write on.

- Once you have a range of ideas, develop blog post titles, or even short summaries of different ideas that you can write about. Techniques such as mind mapping can help, but also develop the habit of noting down ideas from the media, as well as from everyday conversations and incidents.

- Plan how often you will blog, and work out how many ideas you will need to come up with to cover the next few weeks. Then, book in time for another session to generate more ideas. Make sure you have fun with different ways to blog, including using photos, video and podcasts. It makes your site more interesting for your readers.

Chapter Five

Community and Blogging

In the mid-90s, blogging started based on the idea of an interactive online diary: the author writes the entries and readers are free to comment. Blogging has always been about community, and while there have been many developments over the past decade or so, the idea of sharing and interaction remains at the core of blogging, whether it's a hobby blog or a business blog.

In this chapter you will learn how to help people consume your content, how to easily manage the blogs you want to read, how to best promote your blog, how to encourage comments and other ways to interact with your audience.

Blog etiquette

When you first start to blog, you may worry about doing the right thing and want to avoid making a fool of yourself or offending people. On the whole the blogosphere is a pretty friendly place, but there are a few things you can do to avoid conflict or embarrassment.

Do not 'flame'

'Flaming' is when a person purposely visits several blogs and leaves inflammatory comments. This is also known as 'trolling'.

Only leave links in comments if relevant and necessary

Some bloggers prefer you not to leave links to your own posts in their comments as your name acts as a link back anyway. However, the general consensus is that as long as you are leaving a valid comment and the link is relevant then it's fine.

'The idea of sharing and interaction is at the core of blogging.'

Be generous with your links

Linking out to other blogs in your niche will help you to become established and a part of the community. You can do this via a 'blogroll', a list of friends' blogs.

Do not plagiarise

Plagiarism is the act of stealing someone's work and passing it off as your own. Plagiarising is against the law just as much with blogs as with other published work.

Give credit

'Some bloggers have been unprepared for the intensity and attention a controversial post can bring.'

The blogosphere encourages discussion and bloggers will often take someone else's idea and build upon it. If you decide to quote someone or take an idea to build upon you need to give credit to that person in the form of a link. (See chapters 2, 3 and 4 for details on how to link.)

Be aware that a controversial article is likely to spark a heated debate

Controversy can be a good thing, especially if it sparks healthy debate. Unfortunately, some bloggers have been unprepared for the intensity and attention a controversial post can bring, so if you are planning to tackle a controversial topic, be prepared. Try to stay on topic and back up your argument with facts or personal experience. Moderate comments to ensure that personal attacks and off-topic accusations are filtered out.

Disclosure

The law dictates that where your views may be influenced due to remuneration that you need to disclose this. This is most likely to happen if you are sent a product to review or you are paid to write about something. In these posts you simply need to put something like 'sponsored post' at the top or bottom. Bloggers can feel that everyone within their niche is representing that niche and poor behaviour can reflect badly on the niche as a whole.

An interactive blog

Bloggers love comments but comment numbers have dwindled since the social networking sites Facebook and Twitter have become popular. Commenting is a great way to become known in your niche and build relationships.

First you need to find a selection of blogs that you are interested in reading. You can search in Google for topics that interest you or you can seek out top blogger lists to pick from.

An easy way to keep up with all your blogs is to sign up to a reader. A reader will collect posts from all the blogs you subscribe to and collate them so you can read them all in the same website. This process is called RSS which stands for 'really simple syndication'. You can help people consume your content by providing an RSS feed. Some blogs have buttons built in to deal with this. If not you can 'burn a feed' by signing up for an account at Google feedburner. You can also get RSS buttons for your blog from Google feedburner as well as HTML code to allow your readers to set up your blog as an email subscription.

Offer an email subscription option on your blog. This is handy for readers who do not understand RSS or do not use it. Posts are delivered direct to the subscriber's inbox and subscribers are then more likely to come back to your blog. This all helps to build loyalty to your blog and turns passing readers into subscribers.

Blogging is not a solitary activity, unless you want it to be. You can connect with other bloggers through commenting on sites like Twitter and Facebook and by participating in group activities like blog carnivals. A blog carnival is a regularly scheduled event where the niche will come together to share their best posts. Each blogger will usually take a turn to host the carnival. Participants will submit their best blog post on the theme and the host will collate them all into one 'carnival post'. Participants will usually promote the carnival post on their blog and on social media sites. Participating in a carnival is a chance for you to get a link back, 'meet' other bloggers in your niche and promote your post. As a host, you will often receive lots of incoming links as well as a spike in traffic on carnival day as readers are directed to your blog.

'A blog carnival is a regularly scheduled event where the niche will come together to share their best posts.'

Promoting your blog

In this section we are going to look at the various ways you can promote your blog. We've already covered blog carnivals and these are a great way to get to know other bloggers in your niche. Now we are going to look at competitions, joining groups and social media sites that can help you raise your profile and increase your traffic.

Competitions

Competitions are a great way to raise the profile of your blog and increase your traffic whilst also giving something back to your audience.

Running a competition takes a little work, but it is usually worth the effort. First you need to have a prize. You could buy a prize, but more often you will offer something you have been given to review or a product you have been sent to give away as a prize. Do not forget to disclose if your prize is coming from a third party; you will probably want to promote that company or service anyway in return for the prize.

Next, you need to decide what the reader must do to enter. Popular choices include:

- Answering a question.
- Commenting on the post.
- Signing up to your newsletter.
- Retweeting your post on Twitter.
- Writing a post about your competition.

Decide what you want to achieve from the competition; is it more readers? Comments? Subscribers to your newsletter? Once you have decided you can choose the type of entry format that will most likely help you meet your objective.

Decide whether your competition is open to local, national or international residents. If your prize is coming from a third party, ask them where they'll be able to ship to. Always say who can enter, even if it's open to everyone.

Decide on a date the competition will close and make this clear in your post.

Decide how a winner will be picked: a correct answer or at random. Many online competitions are drawn at random using a tool like random number generator.

Once the competition is closed pick a winner and email them. You will probably require a shipping address for the prize.

Joining groups

Whatever your niche, part of the fun of blogging is connecting with like-minded people that share the same interests and passions as yourself. Here are some groups; search on the Internet and you will find many more:

BritMums – A social network for all British parent bloggers. It acts as a hub for the whole community and at last count has over 3,000 members.

BlogHer – An international blog network for females. BlogHer holds a conference in America every year which it has become famous for, they also run an ad network. If you want to network with a wider demographic, BlogHer is a great way to start.

Private groups

Private groups are those that are invitation only. These can take the form of a social network, like BritMums but much smaller. There are a number of reasons you may wish to form or join a private group:

- Network with like-minded bloggers.
- Form a local group so that you can discuss local issues and arrange meet-ups.
- Mastermind groups to share expertise.
- Groups based on specific interests i.e. running, crafts, gaming.

Social bookmarking sites

Social bookmarking is a way for bloggers and Internet users in general to save and share links to interesting articles, sites, photos and blog posts.

Being 'bookmarked' by people on these sites can result in a lot of traffic being sent to your blog. This is especially the case if the social bookmarking site has an element of voting, where users vote in favour of top content. This is how sites like Digg, Reddit and Kirtsy function. Leader boards of content are created with the most popular content at the top. A front page link on Digg can result in hundreds of thousands of visitors to your blog.

StumbleUpon allows users to 'favourite' content and the amount of 'thumbs up' a site or piece of content gets the more that piece of content is promoted by Stumble Upon. This voting system means that some pieces of content can go viral, driving thousands of new visitors to your blog.

Email lists

An email list is a collection of people that have opted in to receive correspondence from a business or individual. In this case it will likely be a list of your most loyal and engaged readers.

You may wonder why you want to build an email list if you already have a blog. An email list gives you the ability to offer more specific content to certain sections of your audience, you may even decide to start a newsletter and we'll cover this later on in the chapter.

To start building an email list you need an email service provider (ESP). You can search in a search engine for email service provider. Popular choices include MailChimp, AWeber and Constant Contact. Once you have signed up with an ESP and followed the instructions, you will reach a point where you are able to get code for a sign-up form template which you can paste into your blog or website. When someone signs up their email address and details are captured by the ESP, you are then free to send emails which are known as either broadcasts or follow-ups from the dashboard of your ESP.

A broadcast is an email that you send to your entire list at the same time. So this could be news of a time-sensitive nature or notice of an event.

A 'follow-up' is an email that is sent as part of a sequence to members depending on when they signed up. This is how you can deliver an eCourse or a series of further articles in your specialised area.

Building your email list

First of all you need to create your sign-up form in your ESP dashboard and paste the template into a prominent area of your blog. This could be on a page of its own, in a post, or in the sidebar. You can put the sign-up form in several places and you can even analyse statistics (in your ESP dashboard) as to which method is converting the best.

Let your potential subscribers know what they can expect to receive when they sign up, for example, a monthly newsletter, 6-week eCourse etc. Consider offering a sign-up bonus such as a free eBook or a prize for the 100th subscriber. Promote your email list on your blog, on Twitter and on any other social media sites you frequent. Encourage your network to spread the word for you.

Tell potential sign-ups that their email address is protected, you will not pass it on to anyone else and that they are free to unsubscribe at any time. It is better to have a small band of loyal subscribers keen to consume your content, rather than hundreds of disinterested ones.

'The best newsletters become a catch-all for information.'

Once you have subscribers you need to start delivering value as soon as possible. Subscribers will unsubscribe *very quickly* if you do not make good on any promises you have made. Aim to under promise and over deliver and you should see your email list grow over time.

No matter how good your offering there will always be some 'unsubscribers'. Maybe someone has signed up by accident, misinterpreted your offer or simply doesn't have the time to consume or take action on the content you are delivering. That is absolutely fine; you only want people who can really benefit from your offering on your list. However, if you notice that you are losing a lot of subscribers, then you are either under delivering, or your offer does not describe well enough what you are offering.

Newsletters

An email newsletter is a regular piece of email correspondence that is designed to keep your reader abreast of news and goings-on related to you, your blog and the niche in general. The best newsletters become a catch-all for information that subscribers eventually feel they can't live without. It is entirely up to you how often you decide to deliver your newsletter, but it can be time-consuming, so monthly is probably manageable to begin with. Use your newsletter to drive traffic to your blog or other online projects, do this by embedding link backs within your newsletter. Build loyalty by offering unique content and special offers to the most engaged section of your audience. You can monetise your newsletter by selling private advertising slots or embedding affiliate links.

Other ways to promote your blog

Guest posting

Guest posting is when you write a post for another site, usually within your own niche. You may be wondering why you'd 'waste' your own valuable content on someone else's blog; wouldn't that just help the other blog rather than your own? In fact it does the exact opposite; by guest posting your best content on someone else's blog you are catching the attention of a whole new audience, some of which will be drawn back to your own blog to read some more of this amazing content. By making sure that there is a few great posts on the front page of your own blog you are almost guaranteed to grab some new subscribers. You can also invite guest posts on your own blog.

Email signatures

Put your blog link in the signature of your emails. Every time you send an email you will be sharing your blog URL with that person.

Forum signatures

If you are a member of fora related to your niche, you can add your blog URL to your forum signature. This means that every time you leave a comment or start a thread, you are also sharing your blog with everyone that reads it.

Quick action checklist

- Find blogs in your niche.

- Sign up to a reader and start leaving comments on other blogs.

- Burn a feed and ensure your blog has an RSS button.

- Promote your blog by running competitions, joining groups and using email/ forum signatures.

- Build audience engagement by building an email list and offering a newsletter.

Summing Up

■ In this chapter we've covered how to become a part of your blogging community as well as how to grow your own readership. Blogging is a 'social media' and reading blogs and interacting with your readers is really important. Now is the time to find other blogs in your niche. Check-in regularly, whether using an RSS reader, or by subscribing to other people's feedburner. Leave relevant comments as a way to ensure that you start to develop a relationship with other bloggers.

■ Building an email list and delivering a weekly or monthly newsletter allows you to build a closer relationship between you and your audience. What is more, it is a great way to promote your blog and get people to visit again and again. Pick ideas from this chapter and do something to promote your blog every week.

Chapter 6

Style and Structure for Successful Blogging

It must be easy to write for a blog, right?

If you have tried blogging, you have probably found that there is more to a good post than meets the eye. Online writing can be quite different to what works well in print. People tend to have a shorter attention span online, so you need to make the most of the different ways to structure and break up your text.

In this chapter, you can learn how to use bullets, lists and links and adapt your writing style to make your blog a great reader experience. Beyond great grammar though, there is much more to writing for a blog. First in this chapter, we look at developing your own voice as a writer.

Writing for the Internet

If you feel that you have lots to say, but aren't quite sure whether your writing style is up to scratch, the first thing you need to start doing is to just write. In the blogosphere, many people are interested in great content rather than perfect grammar and spelling. However there are lots of simple tips that will help you make your writing more readable and compelling for your blog visitors.

Writing style

When you are writing, your first aim should be to be clear for all your readers. Use short sentences instead of long ones; can you replace a comma with a full stop if your sentences are getting long? Write in your own style if you are blogging for a personal or hobby blog. If you are writing for a business audience, either for your own business or as a professional blogger, consider the target audience. A site aimed at academics might use longer, wordier articles, whereas a site for busy mums could use a fun style with short items.

Keep it simple

If you want to get something across clearly online, you need to keep it short and simple. That means that long flowery prose may not work. As a blogger, if you are blogging personally or about a hobby, you know best what you want to say and you may not worry how easy it is for readers, but if you have a business message to communicate or are blogging as a paid job, keep what you write short and cut out extra adjectives.

Draw people in

If readers do not like your blog, there are millions of others that they can view, so you need to grab your reader and keep them there. Use links within your article to draw readers to other relevant articles in your blog – you will be keeping them on your site while they remain interested.

'If you want to get something across clearly online, you need to keep it short and simple.'

Read, review and learn

Learn to take a step back and look at your own writing with an independent eye. If you have written a passionate post, leave it in draft form for 24 hours and reread it to see if readers will get exactly the message you wanted to convey.

Write regularly, reread what you have written and read other bloggers' posts. As you do, you will develop more and have more idea about what is readable, what attracts comments and what captivates your audience. Read books and blogs about writing too, as great input will help your output. Any writer or blogger can continually improve their writing with practice.

Quick guide to grammar for non-writers

Blogging is not just for grade A students who excel at the English language. Good writing helps, but you simply need to create content that is clear and appealing to readers. Grammar is there so that everyone writes according to the same rules and creates a common understanding. If you are unsure about grammar, here are some quick rules to remember:

Nouns are words that describe the name of an object, place, person, animal or concept. There are common nouns and proper nouns, which are names of people or places and start with a capital.

Pronouns are words like: I, me, you, he, she, it, used in place of a noun. In this group you can also find:

- Demonstrative pronouns: these, those.

- Indefinite pronouns: everyone, someone, all, many.

- Interrogative pronouns: who? What?

- Possessive pronouns: mine, ours, his, hers, theirs.

- Reflexive pronouns: myself, himself, herself.

- Relative pronouns: whom, which.

Prepositions go before a noun, and link it to a verb. Examples include:

- In
- Through
- On
- At
- With
- In
- As
- By
- To
- From

Conjunctions join words. For example:

- And
- Or
- But
- When
- Since
- As

Adjectives are words that describe a noun and include colours. You can spot adjectives as they often have endings like:

- -ing
- -less
- -y
- -ful

Verbs are 'doing' or 'being' words that convey an action. The basic 'infinitive' form of a verb is 'to blog' and you can then use the verb in different forms:

- I blog.
- You blog.
- She blogs.
- He blogs.
- We blog.
- They blog.

And aspect, in time:

- I blogged.
- I used to blog.
- I am blogging.
- I have blogged.

ADVERBS describe a verb. Adverbs often end in -ly, but there are other endings. For example:

- She blogs clearly.
- He writes interestingly.

As well as:

- She writes well.

Punctuation

Punctuation helps people understand your writing and the feeling behind your words. Here are some key elements of punctuation;

Full stop	.	Ends a sentence.	
Comma	,	Helps guide your reader through your sentences, shows where to pause, and should be used before speech and quotes.	
Semicolon	;	To link two separate sentences that are closely related, or could stand alone as separate sentences. Used in lsts that already contain commas.	E.g. Jane initially wrote a blog; she the moved to feature writing for magazines. *E.g. Harry Potter and The Philosopher's Stone,* written by JK Rowling; *The Chronicles of Narnia*, by CS Lewis; *Horrid Henry*, by Francesca Simon and *Diary of a Wimpy Kid*, by Jeff Kinney, are all best-selling children's books
Colon	:	Shows the start of a list, and can be used before a subtitle, summary or quote.	E.g. *Blogoburbia: Tales from a Small Town* E.g. For example: pens, pencils, rulers, rubbers, calculators etc.

Brackets	( )	Used to enclose an idea, clarification or additional information. If you use lots of brackets, try rewriting your post without them as this can often make things clearer.	
Apostrophe	'	Shows where 2 words run together. Also used to show ownership	*e.g. wouldn't, can't* *e.g. Jane's blog, the women's blogs* *NB It's is an abbreviation of 'it is', and does not indicate possession.*
Quotation marks	"" ʼ ʻ	Use to show spoken words, exactly as they were said. Choose between single or double quotation marks and be consistent. You can use the two types of quotation marks to show speech within speech – see example. NB. A punctuation mark goes inside quotation marks unless it applies to the whole sentence.	Use to show spoken words, exactly as they were said. Choose between single or double quotation marks and be consistent. You can use the two types of quotation marks to show speech within speech – see example. NB. A punctuation mark goes inside quotation marks unless it applies to the whole sentence.

Bullet points	▦	Used to break down lists. Especially helpful for readers of your blog to see points at a glance. Use a colon to lead into your bulleted list.	
		If you have a list of words, you do not need to punctuate each point.	*e.g. I blog about:* *my kids* *cooking* *crafts.*
		If you have a list of phrases, punctuate each point with semi colon.	*e.g. This month I wrote about:* *the recent blog carnival;* *the films I saw;* *my holiday in France.*
		If you have a list using complete sentences, start with a capital and punctuate each with a full stop.	*e.g. My plans for next month:* *I've got to do my final exam.* *I'm then going back home and plan to complete my latest fan fic.*

Making a sentence

Apart from short exclamations, sentences usually include a verb and cover one idea. If you read a sentence and it has more than one idea within, you can make things clearer for your reader by breaking it into two sentences.

Writing a title

When you title your post, there are conventions about which words need a capital. Capitals are harder to read than lower case letters so you may choose not to capitalise any except the first word. Generally though, you should put capitals at the start of nouns, verbs and words of four letters of more. Only capitalise short words like in, an, on and the, if they start the headline.

E.g a typical title structure:

- Titling Your Blog Posts
- Treasures in the Attic
- In Brittany

Easy mistakes to make

There are some common pitfalls that you see time and time again. Read this section and you will be able to avoid them. Here are my top 10 mistakes to watch out for:

1. Your/you're: Use 'your' when showing ownership, as in 'your blog' and 'you're' when you mean 'you are'.

2. It's/its: It's is short for 'it is', while 'its' is a possessive pronoun. E.g. 'It's going to be a long day' or 'My blog has rather lost its way'.

3. There/their: 'There' is a place, 'their' is something belonging to them.

4. Practice/practise: Think of advice and advise: practice with a c is a noun, whereas practise with a s is a verb.

5. Effect/affect: Effect is a noun – you can create an effect, while affect is a verb – someone affects someone or something else.

6. Complimentary/complementary: The former means something free, while the latter is something that fits well with something else.

7. Loose/lose: 'Loose' is an adjective, a word that describes a noun 'my tooth is loose', 'there is a tiger on the loose', and 'lose' is a verb, 'to lose your tooth', 'I always lose my tiger'.

8. i.e./e.g. i.e. means 'that is', where as e.g. means 'for example'.

9. Could of, would of/could have, would have: Never write 'could of' – the correct English is could have. This applies for would, should, etc.

10. A company is always singular e.g. 'Dickens and Jones is opening a new branch', rather than 'Dickens and Jones are . . . '

More simple ways to improve your writing

■ Think about words that you overuse; it is not good style to repeat a word several times within a sentence or paragraph. Try not to overuse favourite phrases – is there a different way you could say something?

■ If using unfamiliar or foreign words, look them up.

■ Be consistent – sometimes there are a couple of options that can be correct, so stick with one, e.g. *enquiry or inquiry, online or on-line*

■ Again, be consistent when picking whether you use British or American spellings and grammar. Pick one and stick with it.

Problems with spelling and grammar?

If you are weak on spelling, there is a spellcheck function in WordPress, or use a browser like Google Chrome which underlines typos and gives you suggestions when you right click as to the correct spelling. This can really help if you write straight on to your blog. Take one step back if you are unsure about spelling *and* grammar and write into a programme like Microsoft Word which has grammar and spellchecker functions. No computer program is foolproof: you will have to use your intelligence to decide if the grammar and spellchecker functions are making good sense.

Length and structure of online articles

Short is good in the online world. If you are writing an impassioned personal experience, feel free to ignore this advice, but in general keep posts and pages to 200-400 words. If you have more to say, break the article down into sections and offer people the option to click onto the next section on another page or post. See chapters 3 and 4 for more about how to create and use links.

Abbreviations

Once you are getting comments on your blog, you will come across all sorts of abbreviations, some amusing, some confusing. Here is a quick and non-definitive guide to 50 common ones. You will find lots of variations on these if you search online and different acronyms pop up, depending on the context:

1. AAK – Asleep at keyboard.

2. AIBU – Am I being unreasonable?

3. B/c – Because.

4. BBFN – Bye bye for now.

5. BF – Boyfriend, best friend or breastfeeding.

6. BFF – Best friends forever.

7. BIAB – Back in a bit.

8. BITD – Back in the day.

9. BRB – Be right back.

10. BTDT – Been there done that.

11. BTW – By the way.

12. CTA – Call to action.

13. CT – Can't talk.

14. CU – See you.

15. CWOT – Complete waste of time.

16. CWYL – Chat with you later.

17. DD – Darling daughter.

18. DH – Darling husband.

19. DNC – Does not compute.

20. DND – Do not disturb.

21. DQMOT – Don't quote me on this.

22. DS – Darling son.

23. DTRT – Do the right thing.

24. EMI – Excuse my ignorance.

25. FAQ – Frequently asked questions.

26. IIRC – If I recall correctly.

27. IYSWIM – If you see what I mean.

28. IMBGO – I must be getting old.

29. IMHO – In my humble opinion.

30. KK – Okay.

31. KWYM – Know what you mean.

32. LMAO – Laughing my ass off.

33. LOL – Laugh out loud.

34. M8 – Mate.

35. OH – Other half.

36. OMG – Oh my God.

37. ROFLOL – Rolling on the floor laughing out loud.

38. SRSLY – Seriously.

39. TVM – Thank you very much.

40. TY – Thank you.

41. W8 – Wait.

'Once you are getting comments on your blog, you will come across all sorts of abbreviations, some amusing, some confusing.'

42. WDYT – What do you think?

43. WTH – What the heck?

44. WTG – Way to go.

45. WTM – Who's the man?

46. XLNT – Excellent.

47. XME – Excuse me.

48. XOXOXO – Hugs and Kisses

49. Y – Why?

50. YW – You are welcome.

Quick action checklist

■ Are you clear about what makes a good, easily readable post? If not, reread this chapter.

■ Are your posts around 200-400 words long? If longer, practise making them into two shorter posts.

■ Are you pressing 'publish' straight away? Take time to reread what you have written before sharing it with the world!

■ Make sure you read other good blogs and learn from them.

■ Check the grammar and spelling guide and make a point of looking up words that you struggle to spell.

Summing Up

■ There are a number of differences between writing for the Internet and for print. By reading this chapter you should have more idea about how to attract and keep your readers interested.

■ Think about how you structure your blog posts.

■ Use links to draw people into other related articles rather than writing a single, very long post.

■ Check through what you write to make sure it is clear and easy to understand for others: good grammar and spelling is an essential part of this.

Chapter 7

Writing a Blog and the Law

Once you start blogging, it is vital to understand a few legal basics to keep your blog on the right track. In this chapter you can get to grips with some of the laws that govern the Internet and learn about copyright, plus get an insight into plagiarism and libel. You can find out just what you can and cannot do with other people's content, particularly relevant if you want to quote or link to someone.

The Internet and the law

The Internet is not regulated or policed by any one authoritative body. Due to its size and sprawling nature, to date it has relied predominantly on self-regulating behaviour. This self-regulating, freedom of speech style approach is in keeping with the philosophy upon which the Internet was born. However there are a number of separate bodies that help to regulate and police certain aspects of the Web. It is beneficial to understand these and how they relate to your blog.

Laws that govern the Internet

- The Computer Misuse Act of 1990 makes it illegal to hack with the intent to commit crime or fraud. It also protects against information being printed on how to gain access to protected information and systems. Fines incurred can be up to £2,000 with jail sentences of up to five years for the most serious offences.

- The Data Protection Act protects the rights of those whose information is being stored. Information must be accurate, not shared and not misused in any way. Make a note of this if you gather email addresses so that you can correspond with your blog followers.

- Privacy and confidentiality on the Internet is a big problem. Some people argue that nothing on the Internet is private and liken publishing on the Internet to living in a glass house. The Regulation of Investigatory Powers Act is the government's latest measure to help protect privacy and confidentiality on the Internet.

The OFT

The Office of Fair Trading exists to protect consumers. Its legislative powers cover trading on the Internet. There was an interesting case in 2011 between the OFT and Handpicked Media, an advertising broker that brings together advertisers and bloggers. The OFT brought a case that Handpicked Media had allowed bloggers to publish promotional material that had not been disclosed as promotional (www. oft.gov.uk/OFTwork/consumer-enforcement/consumer-enforcement-completed/ handpicked_media/). This was a landmark case that caused the UK blogosphere to analyse and adapt its own disclosure policy. Many individual bloggers and agencies have changed their approach to disclosure as a result. Over the coming years we can expect to see more similar cases like this where traditionally 'offline bodies' exert their powers over online issues.

Copyright

When you write anything on your blog that is your own original creation, you own the copyright, unless you have signed a contract to assign the right to a client. This is based in the Copyright, Designs and Patents Act 1988. You need take no further steps; there is no need to register your content or submit it to any organisation. If you have carried out research for a post, keep your research material and date any notes or sketches.

In the UK you do not need to add the © sign or write 'copyright' at the bottom of your text. In the US, for work protected by the 1976 Copyright Act it is considered beneficial to include 'copyright' or ©, your name and the year of publication. There are widgets that will add a copyright sign to your content which can be helpful to make things doubly clear to readers as well as meeting US requirements. Fundamentally, under UK copyright law, other bloggers and businesses have no right to copy what you have created. You can grant permission to allow others to use your content.

What does copyright cover?

Copyright covers all sorts of content, on and offline, including:

* Writing.
* Designs.
* Illustrations.
* Photographs.
* Cartoons.
* Music.
* Spoken word (when you interview someone, the interviewee owns the copyright on their words).

How to ensure you respect other's copyright

When linking

If you want to mention what someone else has written, it is fine simply to describe what they have written about without permission. E.g.:

'I was interested to read Jane's views on the latest Lady GaGa stunt'.

When quoting

If you want to include what the person actually wrote or said, you should ask permission. E.g.:

'Well, I thought it was totally over the top, so I was stunned to read Jane's blog where she wrote, "Can you say that a pop star has jumped the shark like you can a TV show? I'm no longer interested in nor impressed with Lady GaGa's publicity-seeking antics".'

You should also ask permission of the copyright holder before quoting from books, newspapers etc. Most people will not object if you quote a line or two, attribute it correctly and link to the source. Similarly, ask permission before using someone else's images and credit them as they require.

When interviewing someone

Always ask permission to record an interview and to quote what the interviewee has said. Whether you are interviewing face-to-face, over the phone or Skype, make sure you have permission to record someone's word. Once they have made the recording and written up the article, journalists often read back what they will be publishing to the interviewee; this can be a handy way to make sure that your interviewee is happy with what you have written.

What copyright doesn't protect

Copyright does not protect ideas, so if you have a killer idea for a niche blog or article, keep it to yourself until you can put it in to action. If you share an idea with someone and they use it, you do not have much comeback.

Copyright when choosing a blog platform

Most blog platforms will allow you to retain copyright over your content. As one example, this is what Google says about Blogger blogs in their terms and conditions:

'Your intellectual property rights. Google claims no ownership or control over any Content submitted, posted or displayed by you on or through Google services.You or a third-party licensor, as appropriate, retain all patent, trademark and copyright to any Content you submit, post or display on or through Google services and you are responsible for protecting those rights, as appropriate'.

Source: www.blogger.com/terms.g Accessed 14.9.2011

When signing up for a blog, do check the policies on this point. In the past some social media or blog sites have included the right to use your content in their terms and conditions. Most users find this unacceptable. Watch out for 'sublicenses' in terms and conditions, particularly relevant to photo sharing sites, you may be agreeing to allow others to display your images. This is one part of the terms and conditions it pays to understand.

What if someone steals your content?

If you spot that someone else has used your content without permission, which is known as plagiarism, you will find that blog providers tend to be on your side. If you complain to the blog provider they are likely to take down the site that is violating your copyright. For example, within the WordPress terms and conditions:

Copyright Infringement and DMCA policy

'As Automattic asks others to respect its intellectual property rights, it respects the intellectual property rights of others. If you believe that material located on or linked to by WordPress.com violates your copyright, you are encouraged to notify Automattic in accordance with Automattic's Digital Millennium Copyright Act ("DMCA") Policy. Automattic will respond to all such notices, including as required or appropriate by removing the infringing material or disabling all links to the infringing material. Automattic will terminate a visitor's access to and use of the Website if, under appropriate circumstances, the visitor is determined to be a repeat infringer of the copyrights or other intellectual property rights of Automattic or others. In the case of such termination, Automattic will have no obligation to provide a refund of any amounts previously paid to Automattic'.

Source: www.en.WordPress.com/tos/ Accessed 14.9.2011

Google has a similar statement for Blogger. Copyright extends for 70 years after someone has died.

Blogging for money and copyright

If you are paid to write posts for another business, or to provide sponsored posts on your own site, be clear about who owns the copyright. Get legal advice on setting up contracts and see the Copyright, Designs and Patents Act 1988. Join the NUJ or the Society of Authors as relevant; the membership fee gives you access to legal advice.

Watch what you say

'Alongside being aware of copyright, you also need to make sure that anything you write is based on fact.'

Alongside being aware of copyright, you also need to make sure that anything you write is based on fact. This is particularly relevant if you are writing blog posts for money; do not just write what you are told without checking your facts as your client could sue you if they suffer a loss as a result. Watch out for libel: when you defame, or say something that might injure someone, in writing. A person can claim libel if it can be seen that you have injured their reputation. If you want to learn more about law and what you write, there is some information in the *Writers' and Artists' Yearbook* and much more in *McNae's Essential Law for Journalists* or *Law for Journalists* by Frances Quinn.

Promoting your blog

Once you start promoting your blog, you have further legal responsibilities, particularly if you collect email addresses. Under the Data Protection Act 1998 ('DPA') your readers are entitled to know if you collect and process their personal details and email addresses count as 'personal details' if the person can be identified from them. To comply with the DPA, you need to ensure that people register their own names and addresses and 'opt-in' to receiving communications from you. You need to let people know if you will also be sharing their email address with others and give them the chance to say no to this. Also, give people the chance to unsubscribe from your newsletter every time you contact them. If you are collecting personal data you also need to have a privacy policy on your website. Put a link in the footer of each page. Your policy should cover what you will do with personal data. You can get an 'off the shelf' privacy policy as well as website terms of use from www.offtoseemylawyer.com.

Quick action checklist

▪ Get clear about copyright: go to www.ipo.gov.uk to find out more.

▪ Check your terms and conditions for your own blog provider.

▪ Do you collect people's email addresses? If so, buy an 'off the shelf' privacy policy.

▪ If you are quoting someone, get permission first, attribute and link.

▪ If you are blogging for money, get legal assistance to check your contracts.

Summing Up

- The legal issues around blogging, the Internet and, in particular, data protection are complex. You can be fined if you do not comply, so do get legal advice.

- Once you are clear about copyright and providing a factual base for your posts you will be more confident in your own writing, and you will also be more confident if faced with someone who copies what you have written.

Chapter 8

From Blogs to eBooks

After building a successful blog you might think, what next? Do you simply continue with one blog, pick a different niche and start the process over, or go deeper in the niche you are in? Creating a successful blog is just the first step to what can become a whole career. Bloggers have gone on to become published authors and in-demand speakers in their niche. Once you have an audience that appreciates what you do they will often be chomping at the bit for more from you. You can offer extra information via a newsletter and, take it a step further with an eBook or eCourse. In this chapter we are going to cover why eBooks and eCourses are the perfect 'next step' and how you can create them.

If you have a business you can also utilise eBooks and eCourses to promote it online. A short eBook or eCourse can be a sign-up bonus to encourage people to join your email list. This has two benefits. Firstly it gives your potential customers an additional reason to make the commitment to sign up for more information and secondly it gives you the opportunity to demonstrate your expertise. This process also helps you to sift your wider audience from those who are mildly interested to those who are very interested and therefore primed to buy.

'Creating a successful blog is just the first step to what can become a whole career.'

What is an eCourse?

An eCourse is a course that is delivered completely online. In its simplest form it may be a downloadable file of materials or it may be delivered sequentially using an email service provider. A more complex course may involve a membership site, videos, podcasts and forums.

An eCourse will usually cover one subject or topic area and solve a specific problem or set of problems. It can be fixed length, such as 6 weeks, or it can be an ongoing subscription-based model where new content is delivered weekly or monthly in return for a regular subscription fee.

As you can see there is no set format for an eCourse and the best eCourses are those that are formatted based on the topic, the solution required and the needs of the customer.

Why write an eCourse?

eCourses are useful for writers, coaches, professionals and anyone with knowledge to share. Online courses allow you to reach more people at once. Whilst a coach may be able to hold a workshop with twenty people in a specific geographic area, an online eCourse can help them train fifty, a hundred or even a thousand clients at once. This allows them to earn more money per hour. One-to-one coaching can be kept as a high end service, with a higher price point and limited availability. From the client's point of view online courses are usually cheaper as the coach can train multiple people at once, plus there is no necessity for travel or overnight stays. eCourses are often flexible so people can study at their own pace, this is great for parents, busy professionals and business owners. Overall, an eCourse is both efficient for the provider and efficient for the client. Technology has made podcasting (audio files), online video and the ability to run webinars (online seminars) both low cost and easy to deliver, meaning that online training can be as dynamic and interactive as a live workshop.

How to structure an eCourse

The structure of your eCourse will depend on your topic area, the problem you are trying to solve and how your clients prefer to learn. Here are a few considerations:

Fixed time, one-off payment Vs ongoing subscription payment

A fixed time one-off payment course gives your clients the knowledge that a solution to the problem should be achieved in a fixed time for a fixed fee. This is ideal for those with time constraints or a limited budget. However this model means that information can't be added to or updated as once it is consumed, that is it. An ongoing subscription-based model allows you to deliver more material and to keep updating your content as things change. While a subscription model means a steady cash flow it also takes a certain amount of maintenance to enrol and cancel subscriptions. If your topic is one where the information constantly changes or information is endless, then a subscription model would work well. If your topic is one where the solution rarely changes and few updates would be required, then a fixed time, one-off payment model might be best.

How long?

I'm often asked how long an eCourse should be and the answer is, however long it takes to get your clients from problem to solution at a pace that feels comfortable for them. To figure this out takes a little trial and error, especially in the pacing of your course. In my experience, people learn a lot more slowly and can consume much less content over a period of time than you think they can. If in doubt go slow, you can always batch content to deliver in bundles to your most eager and committed clients.

eLessons or eBooks

Will your course incorporate daily or weekly eLessons or would your topic lend itself better to a monthly mini eBook, or perhaps just one larger eBook? Again this will depend on the topic, your clients, and the style of learning that needs to take place. Is your topic best learned in bite-sized chunks with immediate points to take action on? Or is your topic one where to understand a certain area you need all the information at once? Your answer will dictate whether it is a course with regular eLessons that is required or perhaps one with modules and accompanying eBooks.

Multi-media

People learn in different ways and while a text-based course will satisfy some, for others who learn by hearing or seeing things it will fall short. Podcasts and videos are easy and low cost to create and will add another dimension to your course. Multi-media will also increase the perceived value of your course, meaning that you can charge more. For some topic areas, such as art and craft or technology, it may be appropriate to have a course that is solely video based. If you do create a predominantly video-based course, it can add value and usability if you offer transcriptions. If your course requires tutorials then software such as Camtasia can help you deliver this. Camtasia allows you to record your screen and overlay text, arrows and highlight specific areas. You can also zoom in, add sound effects and add in an array of other useful training aids. If you want to record yourself, perhaps demonstrating how to create a piece of artwork, you can use your webcam and then record the screen with Camtasia. Software like Camtasia affords you significant editing tools too that you will find useful when creating video tutorials and producing videos that are sufficiently professional.

Membership sites

A membership site is the most complex style of online eCourse and encompasses some sort of private members' area where training materials can be viewed and where members can interact with each other and you. A membership site may also have features like member pages, photos, blogs, chat areas and forums. You can charge a premium for an eCourse with a members' area as you are offering this range of additional benefits. A membership site is a good option if you are working in a niche where networking and communicating as a group is advantageous.

What is an eBook?

An eBook is a book that is digitally delivered. It is sent, received and read online or via an eReader like a Kindle. eBooks allow the reader to save lots of books on their PC or Kindle making the process of reading more accessible and particularly efficient for travelling. For a writer, publishing eBooks is efficient and low cost. Releasing books in this format means that there is no requirement for a publisher, your overheads are low and your profit margins are very high. This combination of factors makes eBooks an attractive proposition for anyone with knowledge to share.

What's more, you do not need to be an experienced writer to create an eBook. As long as you have a reasonable command of the English language and you have the resources to pay for an editor then you are good to go. If you do not have these things then you still do not have to rule yourself out of the eBook market. Simply record yourself speaking the knowledge you want to share and hire someone to write and create the eBook for you. You can find people to do this for you on sites like eLance and People Per Hour.

Why write an eBook?

There are many reasons why writing an eBook is a great idea. Here are a few:

- eBooks get to your readers instantaneously. With an eBook you do not have to pitch your book, wait to get a publishing deal, write the book, go back and forth with editors and then wait for the publishers to print and distribute your book. You can write an eBook in as little as a few days and have it online to buy in a few hours. It's also great for readers who can buy and start reading your book in just a few minutes.

- You can sell your eBook via your website, using a shopping cart like '1 shopping cart', 'eJunkie' or 'Clickbank'. An eBook gives you something to sell to people that are really interested in your niche and can be the doorway to selling your higher priced products and services.

- eBooks can be just the length you need. Whilst publishers need to have books of a certain word count, an eBook gives you the freedom to write to any length you wish, including very short eBooks. Often eBooks that are given away as bonuses or complimentary with products are only a dozen pages or so. eBooks allow you to provide your customers with added value but at low cost to yourself. Think about it, if you sell something that has multiple uses such as raw chocolate, wouldn't it be an added incentive for the buyer if with your purchase you received an eBook on the *50 Things To Do with Raw Chocolate*.

'You do not need to be an experienced writer to create an eBook.'

- eBooks cost much less to publish than print books . With eBooks you do not have to worry about costs such as stock, insurance and shipping. This means that you can either sell eBooks more cheaply or you can sell at the same price as physical books and maximise your own margins. What is more, many publishers will decline books that they feel are too niche and therefore a bit of a gamble. eBooks with their low overheads and few barriers to market make it possible for writers, business owners and specialists to take that gamble or to fulfil the needs of a very small niche, and still do so at a profit.

- You can link your eBook to your other services. You can create links within the eBook that take people to other parts of the book or out to your main website or other resources. So while the relationship with the client might begin with a free or low-cost eBook, it doesn't have to end there. Building trust and loyalty and demonstrating your expertise via an eBook could be just the first step to a much longer, more lucrative relationship.

How to structure an eBook

Begin by brainstorming all the sub-topics within the topic area that you want to cover. It may help to mind map these or create some sort of flow diagram. If you aren't good with this sort of thing try writing all the sub-topics down on bits of paper and shuffling them around until you have an order that makes sense. Now break this order down into chapters.

When you are knowledgeable in a particular area it's easy to forget that your readers aren't! Help them out by writing a good introduction explaining any jargon or niche-specific phrases as you go.

Break chapters down by using headers and bullet points. If your book requires the reader to take action then perhaps create a bulleted list or 'take action' boxes, you can also direct people to additional resources in this way.

If your topic requires it, provide visual stimuli such as images and diagrams to aid understanding. Ensure that any charts or diagrams are easy to follow though, as otherwise they could end up being more confusing! Similarly, if the topic is complex, do not be afraid to explain it in layman's terms, your readers will thank you for it.

Throughout your chapters, when referring to sub-topics covered in the eBook, make reference to the chapter to allow readers to flick back and forth to encourage a deeper understanding of the content.

Wrap your eBook up well with a good conclusion. A conclusion shouldn't share any new information but should simply recap on what's been covered. This is the perfect place to highlight your other materials and services.

How to promote an eCourse or eBook

Writing and 'publishing' your eBook is the easy bit. What is more difficult is finding an audience who wants to buy it. Of course if you already have a business, a fan base or a database of clients then this is a great place to be as you can sell to these people quite easily. Beyond that having a web presence is key and a blog is great for this. Your marketing strategy should also include social media, email marketing and ongoing offers and promotions. Find new markets for your eBook by considering the various sectors that might be interested in it. Create specific campaigns geared towards this particular audience, use their language and tap into their unique problems and phrase the solution in a way that would appeal to them.

'Find new markets for your eBook by considering the various sectors that might be interested in it.'

Quick action checklist

▪ Think about the problems your audience face. Do you have the knowledge to help them overcome this problem?

▪ Write down the knowledge you have using headers. Create a plan for an eBook or eCourse

▪ Do some research into whether your audience would be interested in an information product of this nature. You could simply ask people via your blog.

▪ If you think you have a viable proposition, go ahead and create your product.

▪ Sell your product via your blog or website

▪ Create and implement an ongoing marketing plan.

▪ Consider what else your audience might need!

Summing Up

- Once you have invested time and effort in creating your blog, you may want to make it cover its costs or generate a profit. This chapter has looked at a number of ways to do this through eBooks and eCourses. What's more, you may find that you want to offer your committed readers something more.

- eBooks offer you a multitude of benefits for what can be quite a small investment in return.

- Create an eBook to build your expertise and to offer as a bonus, or write something longer that can become an ongoing passive income.

- Promote your eBook via your blog and email list. Consider what your audience would appreciate next from you.

Chapter 9
Social Media for Bloggers

'Social media' can seem to be a baffling term, but once you link up your blog to Twitter and Facebook you will find it is a great way to draw in new readers and make your blog really sociable. In this chapter we take you through the basics of starting with Twitter and Facebook as a way to promote your blog and encourage interaction. Plus, for business bloggers and those blogging for money, we look at the benefits of business sites like LinkedIn and Ecademy.

Why Bloggers love Twitter

Twitter is a great way to find new readers for your blog and develop relationships. Here are some short tweet-style tips to help you get to grips with the site:

* It costs nothing to join Twitter: sign up at www.twitter.com/.

* If you have mastered blogging, you will find Twitter relatively simple.

* Choose a username of up to 15 characters, ideally similar to your blog name. We are @AntoniaChitty and @Erica.

* You can create short updates or 'tweets' of 140 characters.

* Tweet about what you are doing, what you have just blogged about, and share useful resources.

* Your messages can be seen by anyone.

* Use someone's '@name' to draw their attention to a message. If you wanted to ask me a question, you would put this: '@AntoniaChitty, can you give me some advice on my blog'.

'Twitter is a great way to find new readers for your blog and develop relationships.'

- If you are talking about someone you also use their '@username'. E.g. *'Had a great time with @Laura and @Tara today. Hope to catch up again soon.'*

- Use '@name' to send someone a direct or private message.

- You can 'follow' other members and their tweets will appear in your Twitter stream.

- You gather followers by following others who may then follow you back.

- Feel free to join in conversations on relevant topics and meet new people.

- You read messages as they pop up in real time in your Twitter stream.

- You can download widgets to add to WordPress blogs that tweet titles and links to your blog posts automatically.

- A hash tag is a word or phrase with a # preceding it. It helps people find posts on a theme.

If you were using hashtags for a tweet about this book you might say, *'Just reading Blogging: The Essential Guide #blogging #greatbooks'*.

Or, if visiting an exhibition, you might tweet, *'Loving the new Warhol exhibition #modernart'*.

Do not include spaces in hashtags.

Get more followers

Add a button to your blog which will take readers to your Twitter page where they can follow you. You can also follow anyone that follows you. Some of the people you follow will follow you back.

If you follow someone and then find that their tweets are not of interest, simply visit their profile and click 'unfollow'.

Adding social media share buttons to WordPress and Blogger

With personal recommendations being a powerful part of any publicity policy, it makes sense to provide your readers with an easy way to share your posts with their preferred social media networks. Web developer Mandy Taylor of Tame Techy (www.tametechy.com) shares some easy ways of doing this with both WordPress and Blogger.

Blogger

Most Blogger templates will show social media share buttons by default. If yours doesn't, or if you have inadvertently turned them off, you can turn them on by completing the following instructions:

1. Choose the 'design' tab from your Blogger dashboard.

2. Choose 'layout' from the design menu.

3. Find the area in your template where your blog posts are displayed, and choose 'edit'.

4. In the post page options form, place a tick in the 'Show share buttons' option.

5. 'Save' the new setting.

WordPress

WordPress.com sites do not show share buttons by default. However, it will take you less than 5 minutes to turn them on and there are more buttons available than with Blogger;

1. Go to 'settings'->'sharing' in your WordPress.com dashboard.

2. Scroll down to the 'share button' section.

3. Drag any of the buttons you want showing on your blog from the available services box to the enabled services box.

4. There are options below the enabled services box regarding where and how the buttons are displayed. You can set these to suit your preferences.

5. Do not forget to 'save changes'.

Self-hosted WordPress

A self-hosted WordPress site gives you the most choice but will involve installing a plugin. There are literally hundreds of plugins that will do the job.

At the time of writing (October 2011) the 'social sharing toolkit' plugin provides a good balance between ease of use and functionality. Once installed, the options for it can be found under social sharing toolkit in the settings menu of the WordPress dashboard. To display the share buttons, only the general settings and the Posts and Pages options need to be completed.

Promote your blog

Twitter is a great way to find new readers. Create tweets using the title of the post and then the URL. Sometimes the URL is too long so you can make it shorter at Tiny URL (www.tinyurl.com).

Link to a blog post once or twice when it is new and do not be afraid to pull up older posts and mention them if they are relevant to news or a discussion.

Promote other blogs

It is almost more important to promote other great blogs than to promote your own when chatting on Twitter. You can do this by retweeting. If someone tweets a link you like or says something topical, relevant, funny or interesting you can either click the 'retweet' button in the bottom right hand corner of their tweet, or you can copy and paste their tweet and write 'RT' before their user name.

E.g. *RT @Erica Marketing Book is selling really well www.aceinspire. com/2011/09/boost-your-marketing-skills/.*

You can even add your own comment:

E.g. *RT @Erica Marketing Book is selling really well www.aceinspire. com/2011/09/boost-your-marketing-skills/ – I've bought it!*

Manage your Twitter

Your Twitterfeed, or stream of messages, can get overwhelming once you get more than a handful of followers. Use a free tool like TweetDeck which allows you to divide your tweets into columns, themed by search terms or hashtags.

TweetDeck can help you:

* Follow your @ mentions and RTs.

* Reply to direct messages.

* Track keywords.

* Shorten URLs.

* Follow Facebook and LinkedIn updates.

SocialOomph is another handy tool with free and paid options. With a free basic account, you can use it to do tasks like:

* Schedule tweets.

* Track keywords.

* Shorten URLs.

* Track clicks.

* View @mentions and retweets.

* Manage and approve followers.

* Send automatic messages to new followers.

A paid SocialOomph account allows you to manage multiple accounts which is useful if you have more than one blog and to delegate account management which is of use if you want to manage tweets for other businesses alongside professional blogging services.

HootSuite is another tool which is set up to allow you to:

* Monitor and post to multiple social networks, including Facebook and Twitter.

* Schedule tweets.

* Monitor Facebook Insights and Google analytics.

'Your Twitterfeed, or stream of messages, can get overwhelming once you get more than a handful of followers.'

Most of these tools also have apps for iPhone, iPad and other smart phones so you can monitor your social networks on the move.

Facebook

Facebook allows you to connect and share photos, news etc. You can promote your own posts on there on your personal profile, but as your blog grows you may want to create a page where fans can find posts and updates.
When starting with Facebook, you need to create a personal profile page.
If you have a personal blog, than simply use the networked blogs app (see below) to ensure that each blog post appears on your Facebook page too. Many people will read your posts when they pop up in their Facebook stream, even if they do not visit your site regularly. You can attract new readers to pop over and visit your site to read the complete post too.

If you are blogging for a business or have a hobby blog that is aimed at people other than close friends and family, you will do well to set up a Facebook business page. A business page separates your personal updates from your blog updates and there are options for local businesses, entertainment, public figures, causes and community groups too, pick which one your blog fits into best. If you are using Facebook for business purposes, the site states that you need to have a business page rather than carrying on your business communications via a personal page (consider whether your blog is becoming a business when deciding where to share your posts).

Setting up a Facebook page is simple. Click on www.facebook.com/pages/create.php and follow the step-by-step guidance. You could put your blog in the 'companies' section under media/news/publishing as you are a micro publisher as a blogger. Choose a name for your page that matches your blog name so people can recognise who you are.

Linking your blog with Facebook

Networked blogs is a key app to help you get your blog content to appear automatically on your personal or business page. Find it at www.networkedblogs.com and follow the simple step-by-step process to add your blog and pick relevant tags (words to describe your blog topics).

Twitter.com can also help you link up your blog to Twitter, Facebook and other social media sites.

Once your Facebook blog page is up and running and you have regular content appearing from your blog on your page, you will find that you attract a few people quite easily. You then need to make a point of going in every day to seek out more relevant people and highlighting your page to them. You can use Facebook as yourself, or go to your blog page and opt to use Facebook as your page name. This means that if you leave comments on other people's pages or profiles, they will be linked back to your Facebook page for your blog.

You can keep people who have visited your site coming back for more by adding a Facebook box to your blog. That way your new posts will appear in their Facebook stream whenever you update. Lots of people keep Facebook open on their PC or check in via their smart phone during the day, as it draws together all the news they need. By having a Facebook page, you are taking your blog to the reader, rather than relying on the reader coming to you.

Facebook is also a great place to find like-minded people, be part of a community, leave comments and build your network. Help other people by clicking 'like' on their posts and sharing good posts with your friends. The more you do this, the more online friends you will build up who will return the favour.

Use the same photos across social media sites and your blog to help build your 'brand'. You will become instantly recognisable by your image alone whether it is a photo or a logo that you use for the blog.

Other important places to be online

Facebook and Twitter are the leading social media sites for any blogger, but if you blog in particular niches you will find other useful sites to link up your blog with new audiences.
If you are a business blogger, join LinkedIn and try out Ecademy and other business sites. Sharing solid business advice and relevant blog posts with business communities can help you build your readership and raise your profile as an expert.

If you blog on music, check out MySpace which has been a place for bands to showcase their work for a number of years now. You can link blog post content across to your MySpace page and back again, drawing in new followers and reaching out to people interested in music too.

If you are a mum blogger, there are plenty of communities where you can add your blog and meet like-minded mums bloggers. Look at Netmums, Mumsnet and Britmums, all of which have blogging communities.

The scope for online communities is endless. These are just a few examples. Start to search on your favourite topics and use networks like Twitter and Facebook to find communities that talk on your favourite topics. Develop online relationships with people in these communities and you will find new readers. You can also develop links with people who will write guest posts for your site, and who will run guest posts from you too.

Quick action checklist

- Join Twitter.
- Join Facebook and create a page for your blog.
- Use Networked Blogs and Twitterfeed to link up your blog to your social media sites.
- Check out which other sites will link you up with people in your niche.
- Visit your chosen social media sites for a short period every couple of days. Leave comments and share other people's posts.

Summing Up

* Social media sites are the perfect way to link up with like-minded people who will enjoy your blog. Try out a number of sites, both big social media sites like Twitter and Facebook, and also small niche communities relevant to your interests.

* Once on a site, get involved with the community. Be generous with your comments, share great links and recommend other people's blogs and posts and you will find that they do the same for you.

* Visit social media sites on a regular basis. Check in every other day at least while you are assessing whether you like and enjoy a site. Use online tools to ensure that your blog content appears on the site, but remember to go in yourself and add extra chat and comments and reply to people.

Chapter 10

Writing a Blog for Profit

How do you make money from a blog? Well it works in much the same way as a magazine or website; you can sell advertising space, sell other people's products for a commission or sell your own products. In this chapter we are going to look at monetising a blog as well as using the skills you have developed to make money too.

Before you can begin monetising a blog you need an audience, also referred to as 'traffic'. It is these 'eyes' that advertisers pay for and the more you have and the more targeted your audience the more you will be able to charge. So firstly your focus must be on creating a blog that has an audience of at least 100 visitors a day. Refer to chapters 1-6 and 9 on how to do this. Once you have built up an audience you can start to think about monetisation. Overall there are three general ways to make money from blogs. Read on to find out more about each of them in turn.

'How do you make money from a blog?'

Sell advertising space

Selling advertisements on your blog is the easiest of the three ways to make money. If you have a blog in a good niche that is receiving stable levels of traffic, advertisers will be interested in reaching your audience by purchasing space on your blog. You can sell a variety of advertising options:

Sponsored posts

An advertiser will either pay you to publish a post that they provide, or they will pay you to write the post on a particular product, service or subject. This is usually for a one-off fee; prices always depend on traffic, the niche and supply and demand. Advertisers benefit from the readers that view that post as the readers trust the content on your site and will pay attention to any endorsements and the advertiser's website will also benefit from the link back.

Banner adverts

An advertiser will pay you to place a 'banner' which is a picture advertisement in the sidebar or header of your blog. This can be paid as 'CPM' which stands for 'cost per mille', you are paid based on the amount of impressions of that advert. An impression takes place each time a reader loads a page. You can work out how much you will earn by checking your page view stats using something like Google Analytics.

The second way advertisers like to pay is 'CPC' which stands for 'cost per click'. You are paid for each click that advert gets.

The third way is 'CPA' which stands for 'cost per action'. The 'action' required might vary from someone signing up to something, downloading something or making a purchase. You are paid each time someone takes the specified action. This is tracked using software that allows the advertiser to monitor where people have come from. You are allocated the actions that have come via your advert.

The final way is a flat monthly, quarterly or yearly fee for placing the advert.

Which payment method is most lucrative will depend on your blog, your levels of traffic and how the traffic behaves when they're on your blog. Do they click a lot? Are they action takers? Are they buyers? All these factors count towards how well your banners perform and the best way to figure what's best for you is trial and error.

From an advertiser's point of view the benefits of banner adverts are brand awareness and driving sales.

Text links

Instead of selling a banner advert you can sell text links. These are hyperlinks to websites or products specified by the advertiser. They are usually placed in the sidebar and advertisers will pay monthly, quarterly or yearly. A word of caution about text links, search engines like Google frown upon the sale of text links as it is seen as trying to work the system. The text links allow advertisers to increase the rankings of their own sites by purchasing link backs from popular blogs. Advertisers will look for sites that have a good page rank (www.checkpagerank.net/), one that is higher than their own.

Newsletter and forum advertising

If you have a newsletter (or a forum, or members' site) you can also advertise on this. A newsletter offers a targeted audience which may command a premium from advertisers. A forum tends to have lots of page views as people view many threads and discussions so they lend themselves well to banner advertising.

Start advertising

You can start advertising by creating an 'advertise' page on your site. This immediately tells potential advertisers that you are open to advertising. On this page you would usually describe what advertising options you offer along with prices. If you want to automate then you can get code from Paypal and embed 'buy now' buttons alongside advertising options.

It's also helpful for advertisers if you have a media pack they can download. The media pack would include the demographics of your audience along with stats like unique visitors and page views. All these stats can be gleaned from a stats package like Google Analytics. For specific demographic data it might be helpful to survey your audience.

To get started taking adverts on your blog you will want to promote that you offer this service and consider offering an introductory rate. Check out other blogs in your niche and see who is advertising with them. You can contact these companies direct and offer advertising space on your blog, this is a better strategy than cold-calling or emailing companies because at least you are targeting companies you know are potentially interested.

Sell other people's products

The second way to make money from a blog with an audience, which takes a bit more work than selling advertising, is to sell products. You can do this in two ways, you can either buy products wholesale or via drop-shipping and sell them on at a profit, or you can become an affiliate marketer.

Wholesale and drop-shipping

You can buy products that your audience would be keen to buy via wholesale or drop-shipping; this allows you to sell goods on at a profit, which you keep for yourself. Buying wholesale means you have to consider how you will store and ship the goods, whereas drop-shipping allows you to sell products and have the manufacturer or wholesaler send them direct to the customer. This means that you do not need capital for stock and you do not have to worry about storage or shipping.

'Affiliate marketing is a popular monetisation strategy for successful blogs and websites.'

Affiliate marketing

Affiliate marketing is a popular monetisation strategy for successful blogs and websites, as once you have the audience it is easy. Affiliate marketing basically takes drop-shipping a stage further. With affiliate marketing you are referring the buyer so you do not even have to deal with customer service. The seller pays you a commission for referring that person, and this is where your obligation ends. Affiliate marketing is great if you have a large, dedicated following in a niche where people like to buy products. Hobbies like digital photography or cycling are good examples.

You can either embed affiliate links (personalised to you) within your content or you can place banners on behalf of that company or product in your sidebar. If the product is new to the market you may create an email marketing campaign. Many companies have affiliate schemes now. These are often advertised in small print at the foot of the front page of their website.

Alternatively, you can join one of the many affiliate networks. These are like affiliate marketing warehouses where you can pick and choose which campaigns to join. Choose campaigns that are well targeted to your audience. Different campaigns offer different commission rates so consider the commission rate and what the average spend per customer might be.

Affiliate marketing networks:

- www.affiliatefuture.com

- www.affiliatebot.com

- www.paidonresults.com

- www.silvertap.com

For information products like eBooks and eCourses:

- www.clickbank.com

- http://www.e-junkie.com/ej/affiliates.htm

Sell your own products and services

Selling your own products is the most difficult way to make money online as you need to bring together a number of skills. First you need to have the talent to create something that people want to buy. You have to have some business knowledge to carry out market research, do costings and write a business plan. You need to have an audience to sell your products to and you need to be committed to implementing an ongoing marketing plan. You are also in charge of storage, shipping and customer service. If that makes it sound like hard work then it is, but the benefit is that the profit margins on your own products are usually higher than if you are selling a product created by someone else.

Creating your own products

The first type of product you can create is a physical one. If you are an artist, it might be paintings or sculptures. If you are a musician, then it could be CDs. If you are a baker, it could be cupcakes.

You then sell these via your website. You can create a shopping cart using a system like 1ShoppingCart.com that allows you to take payments and track orders. WordPress even has shop themes that are easy to install.

Services

If you are a professional like a lawyer or accountant you may choose to sell your services. A blog provides a great base for many service providers online.

Information products

If you have knowledge to share then information products are a great way to share that. eBooks and eCourses can take a bit of commitment to write but they do have very high profit margins as the overheads are low, you do not have to worry about stock or shipping.

Blogging/writing services

Finally, you could use your blogging skills to freelance in this area. You might choose to specialise in blogging or you could offer email marketing and social media management services too. Many bloggers have gone on to become virtual assistants, consultants and professional bloggers.

Quick action checklist

- Build your blog traffic to at least 100 visitors a day.
- Create an advertising page on your blog.
- Create a media pack for potential advertisers.
- Offer an introductory rate to attract your first group of advertisers.
- Consider whether affiliate marketing would work in your niche.
- Consider creating and selling your own products.

Summing Up

- There are lots of ways to make money from and because of your blog.

- In the first place, work on building your blog traffic.

- Then, start with the 'lowest hanging fruit' like taking blog advertising.

- Creating an 'advertise with us' page for your blog is an easy first step to show site visitors that they can have a presence on your site.

- Then, work your way up to more complex routes to make money, like creating and selling your own products.

- You will find that as you develop your blog you will be faced with plenty of opportunities to grow and your blog may well form part of a business for you.

Help List

Blogger

1600 Amphitheatre Parkway Mountain View, CA 94043
www.blogger.com
Blogger is a free blogging platform provided by Google. Great for starting out
in the blogging world and requires hardly any technical knowledge.

Wordpress

www.wordpress.com www.wordpress.org
Wordpress is a leading blogging platform and provides a free hosted
platform through wordpress.com and a premium self-hosted platform through
wordpress.org.

Typepad

www.typepad.co.uk
Typepad is one of the main blogging platforms providing both free and paid for
blogging packages. There is also the option to have a hosted or self-hosted
blog.

Blogging Groups

BlogHer

www.blogher.com
Founded in 2005, BlogHer is now the largest community of women bloggers,
with over 37 million unique visits (December 2011). Provides support, news
and trends for all women bloggers.

Britmums

www.britmums.com
This is the UK's largest and most influential network of parent bloggers, helping, supporting and networking with other parent bloggers.

Useful Resources

Advertising Standards Agency

Mid City Place, 71 High Holborn, London, WC1V 6QT
www.asa.org.uk
This is the agency which regulates all advertising from posters, banners, TV and internet adverts. They ensure that consumers can trust in the advertising they see.

Favicon

Unit 2, Sycamore Trading Estate, Squires Gate Lane, Blackpool, FY4 3RL
Tel: 01253 624740
www.favicon.co.uk
This is a website where you can create your favicon for your site, helping build a brand.

Flickr

www.flickr.com
Flickr has over 5 billion images on it site to view and is a great place to source images for blog posts.

Gravatar

www.gravatar.com
Gravatar is the site to create your gravatar that will follow you around the internet when commenting or post on a blog.

Youtube

www.youtube.com

This is a video sharing website where you can upload, share and view millions of videos.

The Office of Fair Trading

Enquiries and Reporting Centre, Office of Fair Trading, Fleetbank House, 2-6 Salisbury Square, London, EC4Y 8JX.

Tel: 08457 22 44 99

www.oft.gov.uk

The Office of Fair Trading is the UK's consumer and competition authority. They are a non-ministerial government department established since 1973.

Need - 2 - Know

Available Titles Include ...

Allergies A Parent's Guide
ISBN 978-1-86144-064-8 £8.99

Autism A Parent's Guide
ISBN 978-1-86144-069-3 £8.99

Blood Pressure The Essential Guide
ISBN 978-1-86144-067-9 £8.99

Dyslexia and Other Learning Difficulties
A Parent's Guide ISBN 978-1-86144-042-6 £8.99

Bullying A Parent's Guide
ISBN 978-1-86144-044-0 £8.99

Epilepsy The Essential Guide
ISBN 978-1-86144-063-1 £8.99

Your First Pregnancy The Essential Guide
ISBN 978-1-86144-066-2 £8.99

Gap Years The Essential Guide
ISBN 978-1-86144-079-2 £8.99

Secondary School A Parent's Guide
ISBN 978-1-86144-093-8 £9.99

Primary School A Parent's Guide
ISBN 978-1-86144-088-4 £9.99

Applying to University The Essential Guide
ISBN 978-1-86144-052-5 £8.99

ADHD The Essential Guide
ISBN 978-1-86144-060-0 £8.99

Student Cookbook – Healthy Eating The Essential Gui
ISBN 978-1-86144-069-3 £8.99

Multiple Sclerosis The Essential Guide
ISBN 978-1-86144-086-0 £8.99

Coeliac Disease The Essential Guide
ISBN 978-1-86144-087-7 £9.99

Special Educational Needs A Parent's Guide
ISBN 978-1-86144-116-4 £9.99

The Pill An Essential Guide
ISBN 978-1-86144-058-7 £8.99

University A Survival Guide
ISBN 978-1-86144-072-3 £8.99

View the full range at **www.need2knowbooks.co.uk**.
To order our titles call **01733 898103**, email **sales@
n2kbooks.com** or visit the website. Selected ebooks
available online.

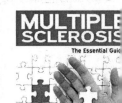

Need - 2 - Know, Remus House, Coltsfoot Drive, Peterborough, PE2 9BF